Home Works

WINDWARD

Editor: Donna Wood
Designer: Marion Neville

Published by Windward, an imprint owned by
W. H. Smith & Son Limited Registered No. 237811 England
Trading as WHS Distributors,
St John's House, East Street, Leicester LE1 6NE

© Marshall Cavendish Limited 1986

ISBN 0-7112-0433-0

Typeset by J & L Composition Ltd
Filey, North Yorkshire
Set in 11/11 pt Garamond

Printed and bound in Italy by L.E.G.O. S.p.A.

Contents

CHAPTER 1

Furniture Renovation	7
Second-hand furniture	8
Simple furniture repairs	16
Stripping wood	23
Refinishing wood	29
Marbling made easy	36

CHAPTER 2

Painting & Papering	45
Surface preparation and emulsion painting	46
Simple painted borders	54
Using stencils	62
Hanging wall coverings	70
Papering a ceiling	79

CHAPTER 3

Upholstery	81
Replacing a drop-in seat	82
Renewing a sprung seat	87
Renewing a modern armchair	95
Making a deep-buttoned headboard	107

CHAPTER 4

Cleaning & Repairing	115
Removing stains from fabrics	116
Caring for everyday metals	125
Repairing and cleaning wall coverings	132
Lengthening the life of your carpet	139
Mending broken china	146
Index	152

Introduction

Every householder knows how expensive it can be to move house and start a new home. You will probably need new furniture and want to redecorate to your own taste. However, buying new furniture and enlisting the help of professionals require a generous budget, but there are other ways of achieving the desired end result.

This book tells you how to find good second-hand furniture at a reasonable price, how to identify period styles, avoid problems such as woodworm and take on simple furniture repairs. It also tells you how to tackle basic upholstery and give an old but well-loved armchair a new lease of life, or give a fresh new look to a set of dining chairs.

Painting and papering are also covered in detail, from surface preparation to applying emulsion paint and hanging wallpaper — including dealing with problem areas such as awkward corners — and techniques such as painted borders and stencilling give you the option to put a truly personal stamp on your home.

Once you have finished decorating and furnishing your home, you will find tips and hints on how to keep it spick and span. Sound advice is given on stain removal and metal care, and clear instructions will help you deal with repairing wall coverings, carpets and broken china.

Creating your own dream house can be most rewarding and needn't cost a fortune. All that is required are a few basic skills, a bit of time and enthusiasm!

CHAPTER 1

Furniture Renovation

Renovating your old furniture is probably the most rewarding of hobbies, because it can transform your home into a dream house. This chapter tells you what to look for when buying second hand, identifying styles such as Regency, Victorian, Art Nouveau and Art Deco, and guiding you towards those which will appreciate in value. Learn how to recognize and avoid woodworm and other problems and take on simple furniture repairs. These are given easy to follow, step-by-step treatment, with advice on how to repair a chair or table with unsteady legs, attend to loose joints and renew badly repaired breaks. In the sections devoted to the various methods of stripping wood, we compare using solvents with the hot air stripper or blowtorch. The refinishing processes of sanding, filling, stopping, staining and bleaching are given full coverage. Lastly, there is a section on how to create a beautiful marbled effect on wood and other surfaces.

Second-hand furniture

Good old furniture very seldom loses its value; in fact it should appreciate in price. If you are interested in buying, look at furniture of the 19th and 20th centuries. Anything earlier would probably be a collector's piece, expensive to buy, and if requiring renovation, would need to be done by an expert to retain its value.

There is a good range of high, middle and cheap quality items available from the 19th and 20th centuries. This means that you can buy within the limits of your purse—but be careful, you may also pay dearly for an inferior article. However, with the advice given here, a study of furniture books and common sense, you should be able to pick up some good bargains. It is worth shopping around to find just what you are looking for.

Where to buy
Auctions: go to those auctioneers who specialize in executor's house clearance. The auctions are normally advertised in local newspapers. Study the piece you want well before bidding, as the auctioneer is not legally responsible for the article's condition once sold.

House sales: all items are sold from the house itself by an auctioneer, or by the owner.

Local newspapers: good bargains can often be found by scanning the 'For Sale' columns.

Antique dealers and junk shops: you can get good value for money from local shops, but if the dealers are in an expensive area, their high overheads are reflected in their prices.

Apart from the fun in searching out lovely pieces, old furniture can be an investment, too.

Dating old furniture
Regency (c1800–35)

Regency is the first of the popular styles and is named after George, Prince of Wales, who was Regent from 1811–20. The overall style is Classical Greek influenced by the East and France.

The higher priced pieces are made of rosewood with carv- ing and brass and/or ivory in- lay, the middle range from rosewood with slight carving to mahogany with some carv- ing and brass inlay. Cheaper pieces can be veneer on soft wood. In this and earlier per- iods, veneer was used for purely decorative purposes,

Carved chair with Regency 'square' look.

not for the sake of economy.

Chairs have a distinctive design with 'sabre' type legs, a broad yoke-shaped Grecian back rail and an overall 'squarish' look.

Dining tables are either oval or round, the tops veneered in rosewood or mahogany, usually with a central leg and curved feet. Other pieces of furniture like sideboards, sofas and the popular Regency convex mirror all follow the same Classical style.

At this time, three important pieces of furniture emerged:

The Davenport, a small, decorative writing desk, with inlay and carving.

The Wellington chest, which is a mini chest of drawers with full height side flaps that lock the drawers into position. It is found in solid ebony with brass inlay, satinwood, figured walnut, mahogany or oak.

The Military chest, which separates into two parts, and came into use during the Napoleonic wars. It has inset brass handles and brassbound corners and is made from a hard wood.

Sofa with scroll ends in French style.

Mid Victorian (c1830–80)

Furniture design became very diverse with the re-emergence of Gothic and Elizabethan styles and the Classical Greek style tailed off. Timbers used were mainly mahogany, oak and walnut, with very little rosewood. Papier mâché furniture was also manufactured, often finished in black lacquer with gilded ornamentation. Out of this period came some popular Victorian styles:

Both balloon back and spoon back chairs are made in solid mahogany or walnut. The beauty of the carving indicates quality, for instance, well-carved cabriole legs would command a higher price than lathe-turned ones. Balloon backs are upholstered so that the material goes over the seat rails—if the legs are loose the upholstery will have to be removed to fix them.

In chaise longues, curved, carved back and carved front cabriole legs in either mahogany or walnut with button upholstery are more expensive than small railed backs and turned legs.

The loo table was named after a card game. It has a round veneered tabletop with a centre leg, usually on a triangular base plus three ball-shaped or 'lion's paw' feet. Some have tilt tops to save space.

The dining table is extended by a geared handle-turned mechanism. Sometimes the table has heavily turned legs.

The Pembroke is a small side table with a drawer at one end and small drop-down flaps supported by wooden, swing-out brackets.

The Sutherland is a general purpose table with a drop-leaf, similar to a gateleg. When closed the centre is often only between 15–30cm wide.

The sofa table has drop-down flaps at the ends, plus drawers at the sides.

Sideboards were made at this time in many different shapes—low or high backs, flat or curved fronts, with or without mirrors, plain or ornate.

The chiffonier is usually smaller than the sideboard with two small shelves on top

Mirror with barley-sugar supports.
Balloon back chair.

and two or three cupboards below, made in ornate carved rosewood or plain mahogany.

The Cadenza is a veneered side cabinet with a central cupboard and curved display shelves at either end with glass doors.

Late Victorian and Edwardian (1875–1910)

Some furniture designers continued to produce the sort of designs shown at the Great Exhibition in 1851. Baroque barley-sugar twists and Gothic arches featured on chairbacks and cabinets, and legs were abundantly curved in Rococo style. These indiscriminate borrowings from past periods resulted in wildly over-blown furniture.

Other designers reproduced classic 18th-century styles, copying Chippendale, Heppelwhite and Adam. These reproductions are usually of very good quality and worth buying.

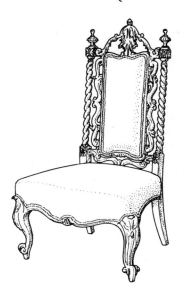
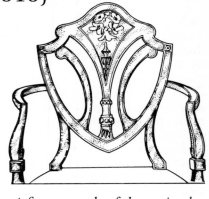

A fine example of the revived classic 18th-century style, in satinwood.
Overblown chair combining Baroque twists, Gothic arches and Rococo legs.

Arts and Crafts (c1870–1910)

Rebelling against the lack of originality in design, and a lower standard of craftsmanship brought about by the introduction of mass-production techniques, a group of artists and architects led by William Morris started the Arts and Crafts movement.

Their workshops produced sturdy, straight-sided furniture, often decorated with hand-wrought metalwork (usually brass, the hinges being particularly ornate). Exotic wood inlays were also used and cabinets sometimes featured insets of leaded coloured glass or fretwork in the shape of hearts or simple flowers. The woods used are oak, elm, ash and walnut.

An offshoot of this movement was the Cotswold School of craftsmen, started by two former members, Barnsley and Gimson. Much of their work is distinguished by the use of black and white chequered inlay, particularly bordering drawers and doors, and the English timbers they used.

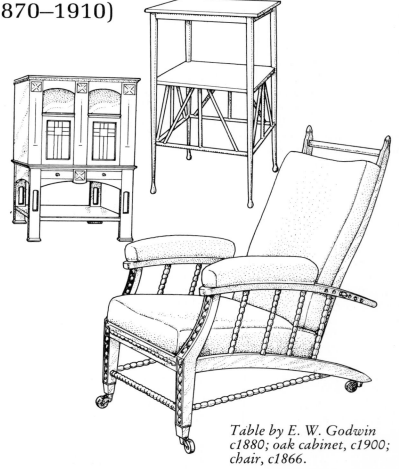

Table by E. W. Godwin c1880; oak cabinet, c1900; chair, c1866.

Art Nouveau (c1889–1920)

While the Arts and Crafts movement was exerting its influence, another style was introduced at the Paris Exhibition of 1889—Art Nouveau. This was taken up in many countries and had a short but pronounced effect on the British market.

In contrast to the straight lines of Arts and Crafts furniture, Art Nouveau was generously curved, inspired by the forms of nature: the curves and swirls of leaves, flowers, insects and human figures. These decorative features were sometimes carved (a small amount of applied carving to door panels etc), but more generally they were achieved by inlays and veneers. A great variety of materials were employed.

Cabinets with glass panels were also decorated with swirling flowers. Metal hinges, escutcheons etc—were used freely and could be made in a wide variety of materials like hammered, wrought iron, brass or copper.

Both the Art Nouveau and the Arts and Crafts movements produced beautiful furnishings, and if you are lucky enough to find them, they are good investments.

Art Nouveau carving on cabinet, drawer handle and three-legged stand.

Art Deco (c1920–35)

Though the Art Deco style followed on from Art Nouveau, it was in complete contrast. Designs were restrained, the emphasis being on elegance and proportion. Art Deco furniture has been described as 'the creation of new forms, using new materials, searching for beauty in utility'. The furniture was either angular and chunky, particularly chairs, or gently flowing curves, some designs showing an African or Aztec influence.

On high quality furniture, some of the new materials used were shark skin, leather and silk, with ivory inlay. Tubular, chromium-plated steel was used for the first time and opaque, coloured lacquers featured.

During one stage, designers 'disguised' various pieces of furniture: radios were made to look like cocktail cabinets, cigarette lighters to look like

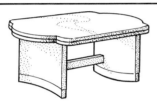

Art Deco table with enamelled top.

statues. Mass production was increasing and plywood was also being used.

As with Art Nouveau, the Art Deco period did not last long but exerted great influence on future designs.

Modern Movement (c1925–60)

During the Art Deco period and for some years after, new groups of architects/designers formed on the Continent, in the Netherlands, Germany and France. Their work became known as the International Style or Modern Movement.

Although independent of each other, their designs were very similar. The de Stijl Group in Holland produced abstract, irregular forms using only primary colours: red, blue and yellow. In Germany the new design school named the Bauhaus was directed by Gropius, who was a pioneer in designing units for mass production.

Marcel Bruer, a Frenchman, came to England, designing bentwood furniture, and in France, Le Corbusier, although principally a architect, also influenced furniture design.

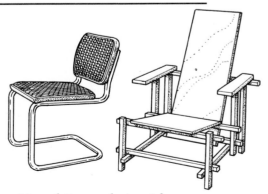

Marcel Bruer chair with tubular steel support; de Stijl Red-Blue chair.

11

What to check

Before you buy secondhand furniture, it is important to examine it thoroughly. This will give you an idea of the amount of work that could be needed—and may put you in a good position to knock the price down a little, or make you decide it is not a good buy after all.

Look for new pieces of wood that might have been let into the furniture at some stage, because these will devalue the piece if badly done. Also check for breaks which cannot be easily repaired, for upholstery that needs extensive repairs, and for signs of woodworm infestation—those pinhead sized flight holes.

If in any doubt as to whether the price is right for a particular piece, seek advice before buying from a reputable antique dealer, or look up the type of furniture in a trade reference book which will give current prices.

Shine a torch in the back of a cupboard or drawers to look for new plywood or repairs.

Chests and Cupboards

The most common fault found here is defective runners that cause the drawers to stick. Check the drawers for unstuck joints or replacement parts let in at the back where they can be overlooked. Make sure there are no broken or missing handles, veneer or beading that you will be unable to replace.

Slide the drawers in and out to check for excessive wear on the runners.

Chairs

The most common fault on chairs is loose joints, followed by badly repaired breaks in the legs, and upholstered seats with broken springs in need of attention. Inspect all the joints, exerting pressure at these points to discover weak points that may cause problems later on.

Place one hand on chair seat, grip back with other and rock back and forth to test strength.

Here the bolt holding the chair together is loose and simply needs tightening up.

Tables

First check the top of the table. Slight scratches or blemishes can probably be removed or disguised, but if there are deep cracks or severely damaged veneer, think twice about buying, however much you like the piece. It could require extensive and expensive restoration work by a skilled craftsman.

Always examine the legs and frame for any loose joints—you may find that they only require a simple gluing job.

Hinged areas can become damaged in time through stress and wear and tear. If the wood is only slightly split at these points, you can repair it without too much trouble. Bad splits mean that you should not buy the piece.

Surface scratches need not be a serious problem; they can often be disguised.

Drop leaf tables often reveal damage around the hinge area; this will need fixing.

When looking at loose leaf tables, pull out the extension pieces to check none are missing.

Mirrors and Frames

Speckling caused by dampness is often found in old mirrors. They can be re-silvered, but the cost can be high. Slight corrosion may be worth living with if the piece is attractive. Look at carving or gilding: make sure it is complete or can be repaired easily.

Missing mouldings and loose joints are two problems to avoid if you can.

Slight speckling around the edge of the mirror is impossible to disguise or remove.

Upholstery

Test the springs of the seat: look underneath to see if the seat sags and sit on it to check springs. Look for damaged fabric and run your hand along the underside to check that the springs are still attached to the webbing and that the filling is reasonably firm and in good condition.

Press down hard to discover the firmness of the interior filling. It should spring back.

Check that springs are still attached to the underside webbing; they may not be.

Woodworm

One of the most important things to check for when buying furniture is signs of woodworm. If allowed into your home without being treated, woodworm can, over a period of time, work its way through other pieces of furniture as well as structural timber, causing considerable and serious damage.

Woodworm is larvae of the woodworm beetle. The beetles lay eggs (about 8–20 at a time) in cracks, bad joints or in flight holes from which the beetles then emerge. They attack the underside or back of the furniture, principally because it is unpainted or unvarnished. The eggs hatch into grubs about three weeks later. These tunnel their way through the wood (usually along the grain) developing and emerging as winged beetles about 3mm long, one to five years later (May to September).

Woodworm will attack almost any timber, particularly the softer types, but rarely attack teak or western red cedar. Their presence is detectable by a cluster of small round, clean cut holes about 1–1.5mm in diameter. There is also usually a deposit of wood powder, where the woodworm has forced its way out of the hole.

If the piece of furniture has been moved recently, the fine powder may have been scattered. If possible, tilt the furniture so that the hole is facing downwards and tap gently: if fine powder falls out, the woodworm is still alive inside.

Look for woodworm underneath furniture, at the back, inside and under drawers and chair seats, and don't forget the feet or handles, too. As a very rough guide, if the flight holes are less than a quarter of an inch apart for any distance, the timber is likely to resemble a sponge inside and have very little or no strength.

Beware of furniture where attempts have been made to disguise woodworm attack by filling in the holes—the woodworm could still be alive. This can be very difficult to detect without very close inspection.

Any signs of woodworm must be treated immediately, preferably outside on a windless day as the woodworm killer fumes can be toxic to breathe. If the attack is light, inject the holes with a proprietary woodworm killer, following manufacturers' instructions, then soak all unvarnished parts of the timber with the killer, using a brush or spray and turning furniture upside down where necessary.

Buy a furniture polish that incorporates a woodworm killer and apply this at regular intervals to eliminate further outbreaks of woodworm. Check the treated furniture from time to time to make sure that fresh holes have not appeared. If so, re-treat the piece and surrounding wood to avoid contamination.

Checking for woodworm

Tell-tale fine dust won't be obvious if the chair has been moved about. Tap firmly where there are signs of woodworm—if fine powder appears, treat the piece with insecticide quickly.

Do not buy a piece with lots of flight holes. This indicates that woodworm have been present for a long time; the interior will be honey-combed and weakened. The same applies if you find cracks like this.

Dealing with woodworm

Once you have discovered signs of woodworm, don't delay in treating it with a proprietary woodworm killer. Choose a dry, windless day and take the furniture outside, otherwise open all the windows. Do not smoke or ignite a gas jet while using the insecticide. Make sure you have thoroughly treated the wood before placing it anywhere near other furniture to avoid spreading the woodworm.

WHAT YOU NEED
Proprietary woodworm killer
Proprietary insecticidal wax polish
Rubber gloves
5cm brush

---

1 Wearing rubber gloves, screw down the spout firmly on the can, and squeeze killer fluid into all the holes, making sure that each one is thoroughly saturated.

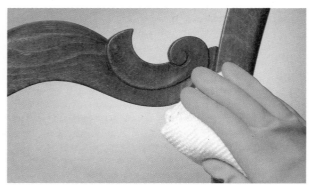

2 Once the woodworm holes are treated, upturn the furniture, decant the fluid into a dish and use a brush to coat the whole surface liberally with the woodworm killer.

3 For added long-term protection, it is sensible to buy a wax polish containing the appropriate insecticide. Apply the polish on a soft cloth once a month and buff as normal.

Simple furniture repairs

Before tackling any furniture repair, assess the cause of the problem, which can include faulty design, the use of poor-quality materials when the furniture was made, bad gluing, constant misuse or changes to the environment surrounding the furniture.

Common problems

Some pieces are so badly put together when they are first manufactured that they fall apart easily after a period of normal use. The wood may be of poor quality and so is more likely to split, while not enough of the right quality adhesive may have been used, leading to loose joints.

With older furniture, a common problem is that the adhesive made from animal bones and skin, used almost universally by manufacturers in the past, has gone brittle with age, resulting in loose joints. Damp will also soften old glue, again making the furniture come apart at the joints. Wood shrinks, especially if it has spent time in a poorly heated home and is moved into a centrally heated one.

Furniture is often mistreated in normal, everyday use: people stand on furniture rather than using a step ladder or put too much weight on only two legs, for example when tilting backwards on a chair. Similarly, old furniture may have been repaired crudely and this may sometimes need correction.

All these simple problems can be tackled if they occur in your everyday furniture or exist in a piece bought second hand. However, never try to repair antique furniture. If you think a piece is valuable, take it to a professional restorer and ask his or her advice—a clumsy repair is likely to detract from the value of the furniture.

Dismantling

Furniture with unsteady legs must be taken to pieces in order to mend it because often all the parts contribute to the unsteadiness. It is unnecessary to dismantle the piece when only one part causes the unsteadiness of the whole—for example, a loose leg.

Always look carefully at the way in which one joint is put together and make a note of how the pieces fit into each other, numbering the individual parts with masking tape. Or, draw a sketch and make a note of any complicated reconstruction that will be needed. It is easy to assume that

Unsteady legs can easily be repaired (see pages 17–19).

you will know how to put something together again, but faced with bits, the sequence is not always so obvious.

Adhesives

Thoroughly clean the joints after dismantling, otherwise grease, dirt and old glue will prevent the new adhesive from penetrating the wood. Fragments of old, brittle glue will prevent joints fitting together perfectly and will prevent new adhesive from bonding. Most old furniture will have been stuck with animal glues and these can be removed by scraping with a sharp knife and sandpapering or by wrapping in a damp rag for a few hours. The wood must be allowed to dry thoroughly before further treatment. Modern PVA adhesives can be loosened by steaming them and then scraping off. Epoxy adhesives can be removed by soaking them in methylated spirits, which will soften them. Other modern adhesives that may have been used for wood are contact adhesives, which can be removed with acetone when hard, and urea adhesives, which are almost impossible to remove except by gentle sandpapering.

Clamping

As the new adhesive dries, the joints must be clamped together, or the adhesive will not bond.

G-clamps are also useful for other jobs such as upholstery and framing, but string, strips of tyre inner tube, or upholstery webbing can be wound round the joints, tourniquet style, to make clamps, while masking tape will hold small joints together until the adhesive dries.

After sticking, wipe off surplus adhesive with wet rag, not with a tissue or paper towel which might shred and leave a messy deposit which would be hard to remove.

Dowelling

You will often find that a segment of wood has broken away from a joint, or that a vital strut or support has been broken in half, or that two different parts of the furniture need to be firmly attached to each other. Never nail or screw broken pieces together or nail parts to each other. Screws and nails hold joins together too

rigidly, which puts a strain on all the joints and looks unsightly. Screws may occasionally be used; one such occasion is when a block is used to secure a joint. Generally, replace broken pieces with a completely new section or, if this cannot be done easily or if the break is not serious enough to warrant replacement, strengthen the break by drilling and dowelling when you glue the break. If you just use glue the repair will not be permanent.

A dowell is a wooden peg used for connecting two pieces of wood, at right angles or adjacent to each other, replacing a screw. Dowels can be bought in different lengths and diameters as well as in packs and they should be a fraction smaller in diameter than the hole they are to go in. When boring a hole for a dowel, therefore, use a drill bit that is slightly larger in diameter than the dowel and drill to an appropriate depth.

Unsteady legs

Unsteady legs in furniture are often due to a combination of two factors. The first is bad design, for example when the legs are far too long and spindly to support the top. The second likely factor is shrinkage of any original timber supports. In cases like this it is necessary to reinforce the leg supports, reglue and repin any other supporting pieces that will help to make the fur-niture steadier, and reposition shrunken pieces. The first task is to take the piece apart com-pletely, removing all the old glue and resticking with a more suitable modern adhes-ive. Techniques for reinforcing unsteady legs include screwing on supporting wooden 'plates' and running wooden dowels from the legs into neighbour-ing supporting wood.

1 Number the parts, then dismantle the furniture completely, removing all screws. Sand the areas to be reglued with medium sandpaper to remove old adhesive and dirt.

2 First glue and screw any side rails back to the top, following the order in which they were dismantled. Remove any surplus adhesive with a wet rag before it sets hard.

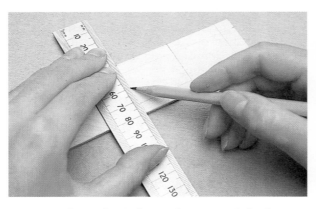

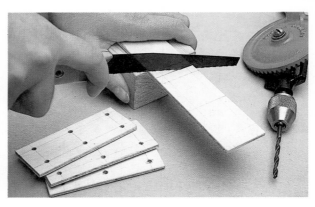

3 To refix and reinforce the tops of the legs, measure out and mark in pencil four pieces of 6mm-thick plywood with 3mm holes in them, and long enough to hold the legs securely.

4 Use a small general-purpose saw to cut carefully along the pencil marks. Support the plywood on a small block of wood while sawing. Drill holes where marked.

5 Glue and screw the cut plywood to the legs, then fix plywood still more firmly to the side rails with 15mm screws. Leave the furniture to dry for a minimum twenty-four hours.

6 To hold an upright firmly where it meets a cross support, clamp the support, a shelf here, to a firm surface. With 6mm bit, drill 4cm holes into edges at each of four screw points.

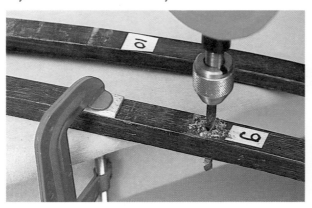

7 With 6mm bit, drill holes into the legs at the point where they meet the hole in the narrow side of the shelf. Make these holes approximately 4cm deep.

8 With the furniture on its side, refit the shelf by gluing and inserting lengths of 6mm dowel through the drilled holes in the legs and also into the shelf.

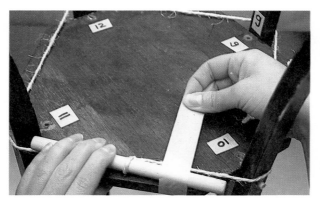

9 Hold in place with a tourniquet clamp made from sisal or thin rope; wind this round a dowel to get good tension. Secure with masking tape. Pad pressure points with rag if necessary.

10 Trim off protruding dowel ends with a sharp knife or a saw. These ends can be stained with a suitably coloured wood-stain to match the rest of the piece of furniture.

Attending to new and badly repaired breaks

A common mistake made by many amateur repairers is to mend splits with far too much adhesive, which simply creates an unsightly bump and does not give extra strength.

The wrong type of adhesive for the job may also have been used. Appropriate adhesives for wood working are PVA (polyvinyl acetate) and urea (formaldehyde) adhesives but people often mend wood with the first adhesive that comes to hand.

Bad treatment, such as banging a gate leg into a stop or standing on tables or chairs is often the cause of damage. Rough treatment can throw a piece of furniture out of alignment so badly that it needs dismantling and completely regluing.

WHAT YOU NEED
Pliers, Hammer
Nail punch, Drill
6mm drill bit, 6mm dowel
Craft knife
Methylated spirits
PVA adhesive
Masking tape
Antique wax
Small paint brush
G-clamp, Hacksaw
Wet cloth

1 Place the furniture upside down on a work table. Protect the surface with an old blanket. Remove screws holding the underframe to the top. For a new break, go to Step 6.

2 If working on a gate-leg table, as above, drive out the pins holding the gate to the underframe, using a hammer and a nailpunch. Keep and re-use pins if in good condition.

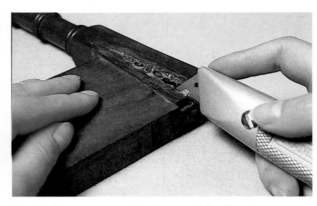

3   Remove any nails that may be hidden in the smashed joint. Pliers or pincers are best for this. If nails are not perfect, they will have to be replaced with new ones.

4   Pick out as much of any old adhesive as possible with a craft knife. The adhesive may be brittle with age, in which case most of it will be easy to remove at this stage.

5   Soak the joint in the solvent for the adhesive used, to remove the rest of it (above, methylated spirits for epoxy glue). When loose, gently prise apart the broken joint.

6   Clean off the remaining old glue with a knife and apply PVA adhesive to the joint. This can often be applied straight from the spout of the container, or you can use a paint brush.

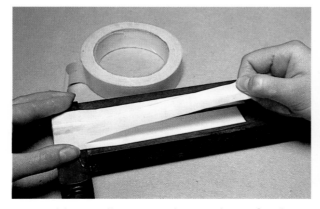

7   Hold a small joint as shown above firmly in place with masking tape until it is dry. Wipe off surplus adhesive with a wet cloth. If allowed to dry, the adhesive will be difficult to remove.

8   Most breaks occur at joints. To strengthen these you will need to peg the joint. Drill two 6mm holes in the joint, each deep enough to get through the two pieces of wood.

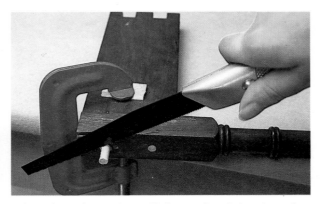

9 Pour plenty of adhesive on two pieces of 6mm dowel and tap them into the holes. Wipe off surplus glue with a wet cloth and allow the adhesive on the dowel to dry.

10 When dry, trim off the ends of the dowel with a hacksaw and reassemble in reverse order used for dismantling. Polish with antique wax and buff with soft cloth.

Loose joints

A common problem with much old furniture is that the joints come loose with age.

Old chairs, particularly, are often roughly treated. People tend to rock back and forth on the two rear legs, which weakens the joints.

It may seem drastic to dismantle a whole piece of furniture in order to restick a few joints, but the pieces are all interrelated. To get a proper balance of all the parts, they should all be cleaned and restuck.

The order in which the sections of the furniture are restuck is important, because although, for example, the back of a chair can be stuck after the seat and legs, stretchers must be stuck into legs, before they in turn are stuck to the seat or the whole piece may not fit together.

> **WHAT YOU NEED**
> **Mallet**
> **Piece of leather**
> **Craft knife**
> **Old chisel**
> **Masking tape**
> **Felt-tip pen**
> **PVA adhesive**
> **Wet rag**
> **Sisal string**
> **Wax polish**

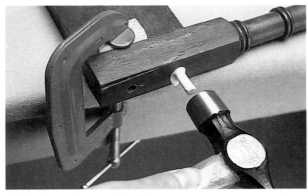

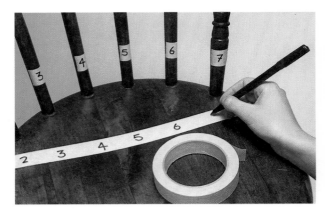

1 Number all the parts on masking tape starting with the top rail, and continuing to the back uprights and corresponding holes, then to the legs, stretchers, and their corresponding holes.

2 Knock the pieces apart with the mallet, deadening the blows with a piece of leather or thick cloth, folded to make it thicker, to prevent damage to the furniture.

3 Clean out the old adhesive from the holes and the ends of the struts and spindles with a sharp craft knife or with an old chisel and knife, taking care not to gouge holes.

4 Apply adhesive to spindle ends and to corresponding holes. When sticking holes, put adhesive on a piece of dowel and twist round in hole. Tap the glued pieces in place.

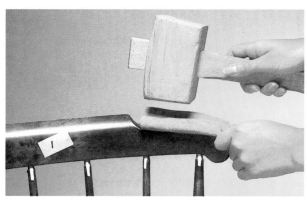

5 Glue the spindle tops, twist them into the top rail holes and use a mallet or wood block to tap them on to the uprights. Soften the blows with leather or a thick cloth.

6 Glue each side stretcher to its two legs and tap them in place, again softening blows on the wood with leather, then glue each assembled side part to the centre stretcher.

7 Turn the piece upside down and stick tops of legs into seat holes. Tap all the glued pieces with the mallet and wipe off all surplus adhesive before it can dry hard.

8 Place the furniture upright on a flat surface with a weight on it. Make sure all the surplus adhesive has been cleaned off. When adhesive is dry polish piece with wax.

Stripping wood

Before painted or varnished furniture, doors and other wooden surfaces can be restored successfully, they must be stripped. This is especially important when the existing finish is either badly marked or flaking.

If the colour of the wood is to be lightened by bleaching, or darkened with a penetrating stain, the finish must be removed first because bleach or stain will only work on bare wood. It is advisable to strip existing paint if a drastic change in colour is being made, because if new paint is applied over old and the surface becomes chipped, the original colour will show through.

Old finishes can be removed by blowtorch, hot-air stripper, alkaline paste or powdered removers or solvent paint removers (liquid or gel type). Items can also be sent to firms who remove the finish by immersion in a hot caustic soda bath—drastic treatment, but labour saving for large items.

Before stripping, the attractive pine table was covered with dirty, scuffed paint.

Methods of stripping

Blowtorches

Blowtorches are cheap to use but can cause the finish to give off unpleasant fumes. Also, extreme care must be taken to prevent scorching of the wood or even fire. Blowtorches should not be used for removing finishes from wood that is to be given a clear finish, since this method easily chars the surface and the marks would show through the finish. For this reason, do not use blowtorches for removing finishes from furniture unless it is to be painted. A special attachment can be fitted when using a blowtorch near glass.

Hot-air strippers

Hot-air strippers are much safer than blowtorches but using them on large surfaces can be tedious—they are quite heavy. There is less likelihood of charring the wood than with a blowtorch, but charring can still occur if the tool is kept in one place for too long. There is also less danger of fire, but it can still happen on certain finishes such as oil paints. It is not advisable to use a hot-air stripper for removing lead-based paints (usually found in older homes), as the lead particles are blown into the atmosphere by the force of the air from the nozzle and can be dangerous if inhaled. When using a hot-air stripper near glass, use the special attachment.

Above left: Blowtorches can be used successfully on anything that is to be repainted, since any accidental scorch marks will be covered over with new paint. Do not use on valuable antiques.

Above right: Any furniture that is to have a clear finish should be stripped with solvent paint stripper. Spirit based solvents are better than the water based ones as they do not raise the wood grain.

Powder and paste strippers

Although this information is not always given on the packaging, powdered and paste paint removers which contain caustic soda are suitable for removing varnish as well as oil-based paints. But they cause many woods to discolour and darken and should not therefore be used if you intend to refinish the surface with a clear finish. They are slow-acting and take much longer to remove paint than a solvent paint remover does. However, they clean out intricate areas very efficiently.

Solvent paint removers

When you intend to apply a clear finish, old finishes should be removed from furniture with solvent paint remover, available either with a spirit or water-soluble base. The article should be stripped in a very well-ventilated room or in the open air. Stand the article on a polythene sheet to avoid damage to floor coverings and remember to wear rubber gloves to protect your hands.

Sanding

In general, finishes should not be removed by sanding, as disc sanders score the wood with circular marks, which show under a clear finish or paint. Also, thin veneers can easily be damaged and many timbers, such as mahogany acquire a beautiful deep colour on ageing and this would be removed by sanding, spoiling the antique look.

How to work out your quantities

A litre (2 pints) of solvent usually covers about 8 square metres but if the paint is very thick, a litre may strip only $5\frac{1}{2}$ square metres. However, French polish is thinner than paint so a litre will probably remove about 11 square metres. A kilo (2lb) pack of powder stripper covers nearly half a square metre and a 1.8 kilo (4lb) pack covers nearly three-quarters of a square metre, each applied 3mm thick.

A litre bucket of paste stripper covers one-third of a square metre and a 2.5 litre (4 pint) bucket of paste stripper covers four-fifths of a square metre, applied 3mm thick.

Renewing the surface

Before applying another finish, the surface may need further treatment to remove stains, deep scratches, burn marks or broken veneer.

Using a hot-air stripper for skirtings and doors

As hot paint can burn, wear strong PVC gloves. Heat the finish with the hot-air stripper held in one hand, and use the other to scrape off the paint, putting scrapings in a tin. It is safest to strip mouldings using a solvent after completing the main surface with the hot-air stripper.

> **WHAT YOU NEED**
> **Hot-air stripper, 2cm scraper, Rags, Empty tin**
> **Protective gloves and clothing**

1   Switch on the stripper, set the lock on the side for continuous use. Move the nozzle back and forth across a small area, say about 10 square cm, until the paint begins to bubble.

2   Work from the bottom up or side to side, scraping off in grain direction, holding scraper at low angle to the surface. Remove paint residues with solvent.

Using a blowtorch

Be careful when working near glass and protect it with a heat-proof pad. You can buy different heads for spreading or reducing flame. Never leave an ignited blowtorch unattended. Keep a bucket of water handy in case of fire.

> **WHAT YOU NEED**
> **Blowtorch, Protective gloves and clothing**
> **Protective heat-proof pad, 2.5cm scraper**

1   Hold flame close enough to paint to soften it without charring the wood. Work on small areas, playing the flame across the surface, and never linger on one spot.

2   As soon as the paint begins to bubble, lift it off with the scraper, working in the grain direction and taking care not to gouge or damage the wood.

Using solvent paint remover on furniture

Before starting, remove all fittings such as drawer handles and steep in stripper. Then use wire wool to remove finish. Protect the floor beneath the piece, and its immediate surroundings, with newspaper. If you use a wire brush to remove the stripper from mouldings, work outside as brushing can flick paint and paint remover.

If stripping inside, always work in a well-ventilated room.

Solvent paint removers do not raise the grain of the wood, so sanding is not usually necessary afterwards. Some brands can be rinsed off with water, others with white spirit: always read the instructions. Solvent paint strippers will remove most surfaces from oil-based paints to old varnishes.

WHAT YOU NEED
Solvent paint remover
Old paint brush
2.5cm scraper
No 2 or 3 steel wool
White spirit
Rags
2 empty tins
Newspapers
PVC gloves
Protective clothing

1 Decant remover into a tin, brush on a thin coat and leave to soften. When the surface bubbles, dab on a second coat to push solvent back on to surface so it continues to work.

2 Test finish with a thin, flat scraper. If it is ready, remove as much as you can, working with the grain. Wrap the scrapings in newspaper or place in tin, but do not burn.

3 To remove any residue from the surface and the grain, moisten wood again with paint remover and rub with pieces of steel wool. Rub along grain to avoid scratching the wood.

4 After the old finish has been completely stripped, wipe the surface with clean rag moistened with white spirit. Water raises the grain so do not use it for rinsing.

A stripped pine chest, given a new lease of life for a child's bedroom.

Stripped furniture

Many people prefer to reveal the beauty of wooden furniture by stripping it, rather than hiding it under thick paints and dark varnishes. Solid woods, such as pine, oak and beech, respond well to this treatment and display very attractive grains.

After stripping, the wood can be left in its natural state or it can be stained, bleached, limed or given an antique finish.

Clear, matt, satin or gloss polyurethane varnishes will show the grain of the wood satisfactorily and provide protection which will last for years, while more ambitious restorers may prefer to try French polishing.

Above right: Stripped furniture with new finishes. The settle has been stained, the cupboard bleached, the chair varnished.

Right: This piece of stripped and varnished furniture was probably once an old washstand.

Far right: A small pine wall cupboard, restored by stripping and bleaching.

Using paste strippers on intricate shapes

These strippers are particularly useful on carved or moulded areas, because the paste, when ready, simply peels off, bringing all the old paint or varnish with it. Any remaining paint or varnish can be scrubbed off with water and the wood lightly sanded.

Powder strippers are mixed with water—follow the manufacturer's instructions. Paste strippers come already mixed. You can use either on varnish or oil-based gloss.

Some woods darken or discolour with these pastes, so carry out a test first on a concealed area. Also, they are not as economical as the other methods shown, so use only for small items.

Remember to protect floor with newspapers and take care not to let these caustic strippers come into contact with skin or eyes. If they do, wash at once with plenty of cold water. Always wear protective gloves when working.

WHAT YOU NEED
Powder or paste stripper
PVC gloves
Brush
Protective clothing
Newspaper
Bucket
Polythene sheet
Stick
2.5cm scraper

1 Mix the paste and, like a poultice, spread generously at least 3mm thick, using the scraper as a trowel. Work well into crevices and mouldings, eliminating all bubbles.

2 The paste needs to be kept moist and left on for at least four hours for the best results. Thick paint may take up to 10 hours. To keep paste moist, cover it with polythene sheeting or household cling wrap.

3 Peel off the paste, using the scraper as a trowel—do this carefully to avoid leaving scars which will then have to be treated. Or, loosen skin at top edge and peel off in strips.

4 Scrub off any remaining paint with scrubbing brush and water. Allow the wood to dry out naturally and thoroughly. When dry, fill any crevices before sandpapering surface smooth.

Refinishing wood

Once the paint has been stripped off a wood surface, it is possible to assess what needs to be done to restore its beauty.

Bleaching or staining often improves the colour of wood but to get a really good result, careful surface preparation is essential. Blemishes revealed by stripping will be even more noticeable when the clear finish is applied to the wood.

Whatever you intend to do with the wood, the first step is to sandpaper the surface smooth. This will enable you to see clearly blemishes such as holes and cracks.

If the wood is open-grained, as is the case with oak or mahogany, it will have to be filled with a special grain filler (available from DIY shops)

Staining can give a completely new appearance to a piece of furniture.

since it is difficult to achieve a smooth gloss on an open-grained surface. If the wood is close-grained, such as pine or fir, no filler is needed.

After sanding and applying grain filler if necessary, scratches and other surface imperfections should be filled with wood stopping.

The final colour of the wood is a matter of personal taste. Bleaching will remove colour from all woods and you can then either leave the surface very pale or stain it. The surface can then be finished by varnishing or you can use a varnish that incorporates the stain.

Materials guide

Sanding

'Sanding' describes the smoothing down of the wood surface, yet true sandpaper is no longer obtainable. Originally, sandpaper was simply paper with sand sprinkled over an adhesive coating, but modern 'sandpapers' are made from all kinds of abrasive materials, from crushed glass (hence glasspaper) to silicone carbide.

Glasspaper is the paper most commonly used for woodworking. It is sold in sheets and is graded from flour paper—which is very fine—to number 3—which is the coarsest.

Garnet paper, made from crushed garnets, is also used, particularly in cabinet making. More expensive than glasspaper, it lasts longer and comes in finer grades.

Other abrasive papers are silicone carbide (wet-and-dry paper) and aluminium oxide.

Hand sanding is for fine finishing on wooden surfaces. When hand sanding flat surfaces, wrap the paper round a hand-sized cork or wooden sanding block to hold the paper taut. Rub the wood only with the grain—if you rub in a circular movement or across the grain, the surface will be marked. When sanding near the edges of furniture, keep the block flat; don't tip it over the edge, or it will lose its sharp angle. Start sanding with coarse-grained paper and progress to the finest grade of glasspaper, garnet paper or flour paper.

Machine sanding can be used on large surfaces.

There are several types of mechanical sander available. Some fit on to electric drills, others are bought as separate electric tools. Both types have abrasive papers to fit. Always finish by hand with the finest glasspaper. Belt sanders are excellent for quick sanding of flat surfaces. They have a vacuum bag attached to absorb dust as you work. Drum sander attachments, which work with an abrasive band, are useful for curved surfaces. Orbital sanders move in an oval rather than a linear way and have a flat rectangular plate, to give a fine finish on large surfaces.

Badly marked solid-wood furniture may need to be lightly planed with a cabinet-maker's scraper—a thin, flat piece of metal (about 15cm × 10cm), with a burred edge. Finish by sanding either by hand or by machine.

Bleaching

Bleach is used to make wood a lighter shade, to change the colour of the wood completely (from that of mahogany to that of oak for example), and to remove small stains like wine or ink.

Never use household bleach for any of these jobs, because it damages the wood fibres. Instead, use a strong commercial wood bleach, which is supplied in two parts. Follow the manufacturer's instructions exactly. One alternative method, particularly effective for small inkstains, but not strong enough for the other bleaching jobs, is to apply a solution of 15ml (1 tablespoon) oxalic acid and 600ml (1 pint) of water. Oxalic acid is poisonous, so handle it with great care and wear protective gloves.

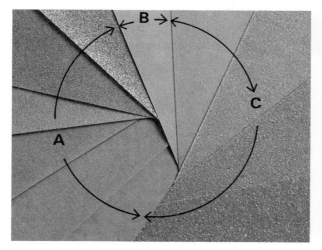

Abrasive papers include red garnet papers (A), flour paper (B) and glasspapers (C).

Wood is bleached with two liquids, brushed on in turn and removed with a sponge.

Filling

To fill the grain on an open-grained wood, either rub in a grain filler (available from DIY shops) or apply many coats of varnish, sanding down lightly between coats.

Use a filler that matches the colour of the wood as closely as possible. Natural-coloured grain filler, which is thinned with white spirit, can be tinted by adding a wood stain, also thinned with white spirit. Apply according to the manufacturer's instructions. Because grain filler shrinks use stopping rather than filler for filling holes.

Stopping

To fill cracks and holes or sunken screw heads, use wood stopping. Several brands are available from DIY shops. Apply with a knife and leave to dry—stopping sets quickly. If a large hole is being stopped, you may have to apply two layers as the stopping may shrink.

Stopping will always show through a clear finish because it breaks the pattern of the grain. Use one nearest to the shade of the wood being treated—some of the stopping shades available are shown right. Fill proud and sand the stopping until flush with the surface.

Filling colours (left to right): mahogany; oak teak; natural.

Stopping colours (left to right): mahogany; oak; teak; natural.

Staining

A wide range of woodstains is available based on white spirit, methylated spirit, or water. Water-based stains raise the grain of the wood so allow to dry well, then sand. Mix colours of the same type of stain to get the exact shade.

Apply some of the stain to a small, hidden area or to a spare piece of identical wood to see whether you like the effect. Some woods absorb more stain than others, and the colour will be darker.

Allow the test stain to dry—it will be a lighter colour when dry—then apply a coat of the in-tended finish. This, too, will affect the colour—some woods, such as mahogany and walnut, go darker even when completely clear finishes are applied. For an idea of the colour after the clear finish has been applied, dampen a small area of the wood with water.

Wood stain colours (left to right): light teak; mahogany, red (top) and brown (bottom); Burmese teak (top); ebony (bottom); oak, medium (top) and light (bottom); walnut; pine.

Varnishing

Polyurethane varnish is the most satisfactory clear finish for DIY use on furniture and other interior wood. (Outdoor wood should be treated with wood preservatives, yacht varnishes or exterior wood stain.) Available in gloss, satin or matt finishes, polyurethane varnish resists both water and alcohol.

Varnish stains are also available. These varnishes contain wood colours and can be applied over an existing finish which is clean of wax and grease. Otherwise the wood must be stripped. The disadvantages of varnish stains are that, un-less they are applied evenly, the colour can be blotchy where the thickness of the varnish varies, and that each successive coat makes the wood look darker in colour; this can be avoided by applying clear varnish instead.

When applying either clear polyurethane varnish or varnish stain, use a good-quality varnish brush. Choose the correct size for the job—for example, don't use a 1.25cm-wide brush to varnish a sideboard. Because a varnish brush is expensive, clean it thoroughly with white spirit and if possible, hang up to dry.

Sanding

When hand-sanding, wrap the paper tightly round a block to spread the pressure evenly and always rub with the grain of the wood. Start with a coarse glasspaper and progress to flour paper. If machine sanding, the minimum of pressure is required—heavy pressure will slow down the machine. Before sanding by hand or machine, use a cabinet maker's scraper to smooth badly marked solid-wood surfaces.

> ## WHAT YOU NEED
> **Cabinet maker's scraper**
> **Sandpaper, Sanding block**
> or **Machine sander of your choice**

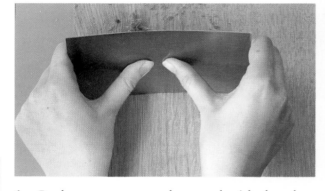

1 Push scraper across the wood with thumbs pressed hard into the back of the blade to produce a slight curve. Remove wood shavings with a cloth before sanding.

2a If using sandpaper, wrap a piece round a sanding block and sand the wood surface smoothly, following the grain of the wood and applying even pressure.

2b If using an orbital sander, fit abrasive paper and secure it tightly. Hold the sander with both hands and keep it moving over the surface without undue pressure.

2c If using a belt sander, move it back and forth over the surface without using undue pressure. Work with a grade of belt suitable for the surface being sanded.

2d If using a drum attachment on a drill, hold it with both hands, as it is heavy. This attachment is useful for curved surfaces, but take care not to remove too much surface.

Bleaching

Proprietary bleaches are usually available in two parts, a pre-treatment solution and a bleach solution. They will produce dramatic results on most woods if you follow the manufacturer's instructions to the letter. Repeat the treatment as necessary, until the wood is light enough. The chemicals are strong, so wear protective clothing, particularly gloves.

WHAT YOU NEED
Proprietary bleach, Two jam jars
Paint brush, Bucket
White vinegar, Sponge
Gloves, Protective clothing

1 Pour pre-treatment solution into a jam jar. Apply solution to the wood with a paint brush and leave it to soak in as recommended. It will make wood darker. Wash brush.

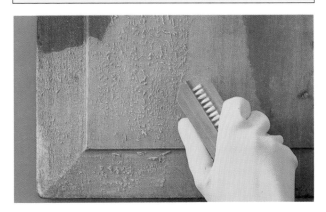

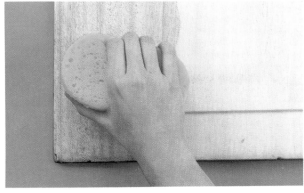

2 Pour second solution into another jar. Apply with brush; leave as recommended. The surface will bubble, then flake. When dry, brush off. For a lighter colour, repeat Steps **1** and **2**.

3 Sponge off all the chemicals with a 50–50 solution of white vinegar and water, applying liberally. Leave to dry very thoroughly and when dry, sand the wood surface.

Filling

If grain is very obvious on the wood, it needs to be filled in order to make the smooth surface necessary for a high gloss finish. Grain fillers can be bought in wood colours or can be coloured with wood stain. Use a filler approximating in shade to the wood to get the best final effect on the surface.

WHAT YOU NEED
Grain filler, Coarse rag
White spirit
Fine sandpaper

1 Apply filler to the surface on a piece of coarse rag, rubbing hard across the grain. Inspect the surface to make sure all the grain has been filled.

2 Remove any surplus filler across the grain with white spirit on a clean cloth, and allow to dry hard. Rub lightly with sandpaper if necessary to smooth the surface.

Stopping

Wood stopping is used for filling in cracks, scratches and other holes. It is usually applied with a knife or scraper and very quickly sets very hard. Wood stopping should not be used for grain filling, nor should grain filler be used for wood stopping. If wood stopping shrinks, apply more.

WHAT YOU NEED
Paintbrush, Stopping
Scraper
Medium sandpaper

1 Using a small brush, make sure the hole or crack is clean and dry. Push in the stopping with the scraper. Remove any stopping from the surrounding surface.

2 When it is hard, remove surplus wood stopping by sanding until it is smooth and level with the surrounding area. If the stopping chips, apply more and sand as before.

Staining

The result of staining depends on the original colour of the wood—the darker the wood, the darker the colour. Before staining, sand the surface with flour paper and wipe clean with white spirit on a soft cloth. After staining, unless you use a varnish stain, the wood needs a final varnish.

WHAT YOU NEED
Clean cloths
White spirit
Woodstain
French polish

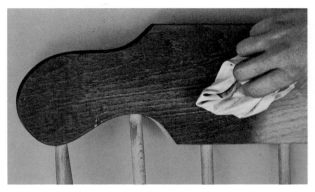 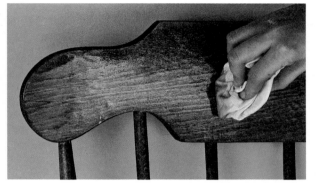

1 Test colour first on a spare piece of wood. Apply stain with a cloth and rub it over the surface briskly, so colour spreads evenly. Dry as recommended on the pack.

2 Seal in the stain with a coat of white French polish applied on a rag. (Otherwise it will 'bleed'.) Apply the clear finish when the surface is dry—check on a hidden area.

Varnishing

Never shake or stir tins of clear gloss varnish. It causes bubbles which are hard to remove. Clear satin and matt varnishes must be stirred until no sediment remains, otherwise the varnishes will dry as gloss. When the varnish is dry, rub with fine sandpaper and wipe clean with a cloth.

WHAT YOU NEED
Varnish, Varnish brush
Cloth, Flour paper

1 For priming coat, dilute with white spirit as on tin. Dip brush into solution about half way up bristles. Apply varnish, working into wood with quick and even strokes.

2 Brush evenly at right angles to first strokes, then diagonally with reduced pressure. Lightly draw brush across surface along grain. Use neat varnish as before for following coats.

Marbling made easy

One of the most exciting ways of decorating your furniture is to create a false marbled effect. Although simulating specific types of marble requires a complex and advanced technique, you can create a beautiful marble-look finish quite simply, by following the step-by-step instructions on the following pages.

The fake marbling process incorporates various techniques: applying glaze and colour; breaking up the colour as you wish, by stippling, rag-rolling, spattering with white spirit (and anything else you like to experiment with); softening; veining, and varnishing.

The techniques of breaking up the colour can be used as finishes in themselves, if you prefer. For example, you may want a stippled or a rag-rolled finish, in which case take much more care over the appropriate stage in the process, leave to dry and varnish as shown. You may also want to repeat or omit certain stages, depending upon the effect you want to achieve. There must always be room for improvisation, since it is impossible to tell, when you start, exactly how the pattern will develop. Adapt it as necessary.

Experiment and practise
The key to success and enjoyment is practice and experimentation. Practise the techniques shown here until you are confident, before applying them to your furniture. A bath panel (available from DIY shops), cut into six manageable strips, provides an excellent surface on which to practise.

Very little specialist equipment is necessary—though it is worth the investment (and specialist brushes are very costly) if you decide to take up marbling seriously. The only vital specialist tool is the hog's hair softening brush which is used to blend the colours together subtly, and avoid any defined colour contours. Without this, your fake

Above: The materials used to marble the table on page 38 were wax furniture polish (1) for finishing off; scumble glaze (2); gloss varnish (3); satin varnish (4), and artist's oil colours—Payne's grey Venetian red (5 and 6)

Left and below: Gather together these items, along with the materials shown above right, and you will be ready to start marbling: white spirit (1) for thinning glaze, making veins, and mottling the glaze; an old brush (2) for applying colour and glaze; hog's hair softening brush (3); a good-quality brush for varnishing (4); waxed 0000 wire wool (5) for polishing varnish; wet and dry paper on a sanding block (6); synthetic sponge (7); feathers for veining (8); palette knife (9)— optional, for use if mixing colour and glaze; chamois leather (10), an experimental alternative for rags when rolling; professional stippling brush (11)—an expensive item which is worth buying if you want to take up stippling, rag-rolling or marbling seriously; rags (12).

marble might look effective from a distance, but will tend to look harsh when seen close up. You can buy specialist equipment from decorative paint specialist shops.

Applying colour and stippling

For marbling small areas such as pieces of furniture or a door, the scumble glaze can be mixed with artist's oil colours (do not use 'student's' paints, since the colour will fade with time). Alternatively, paint on a thin layer of glaze, then add colour (as shown overleaf). For a large-scale work, use a very small amount of oil-based eggshell paint to add colour—one eggcup-full per litre of scumble glaze. Once the glaze and paint mix has been brushed on to the surface, it can be stippled. If you want a stippled rather than a marbled finish, take care to create an evenly-textured surface. Otherwise (if you are going on to rag-roll or marble), stipple the surface more randomly. Professionals use a hog's hair stippling brush to achieve a perfect stipple, but a synthetic sponge bounced upon the surface will create a similar effect, which is perfectly adequate if you are going on to marble.

Breaking up the colour

Once the coloured glaze has been stippled, it can be broken up even further. A variety of techniques can be used, one of the most traditional being rag-rolling. To do this, you simply screw up a rag, and roll it randomly across the surface. You can use anything—experiment by rolling with an old chamois leather or sponge. At this point, you might decide to add more colour (either the same colour, or a different one), and stipple or rag-roll it until you are happy with the surface pattern which has developed. When marbling, you might only want to stipple certain areas, and rag-roll others—feel free to experiment, judging the developing texture and pattern by eye.

Blending and veining

The broken colour is the basis for the marbling technique. First, however, the colour needs to be

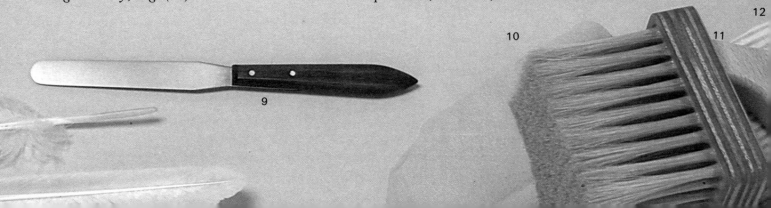

An old table given a new marbled finish.

softened with a special brush, so that each patch of colour blends into the next. After softening, the surface will have a marbled look, but without the veins which characterize real marble.

Veins can be treated in various ways—you can either add coloured veins, or use white spirit to eat away the coloured glaze back to the dried base colour. The tip or the side of a feather can be used for veining.

Finishing off

Considerable time should be spent on varnishing if you are going to give a marble-like feel to your painted surface. A coat of gloss polyurethane varnish, followed by two coats of satin varnish—rubbing back *very* gently between coats with water-soaked wet and dry—is recommended. Once the final coat is thoroughly dry, rub down very lightly with very fine (grade

0000) wire wool, well-waxed with furniture wax. Finally, burnish the surface with wax furniture polish on a soft cloth.

The secret ingredient of decorative marbling is 'scumble glaze'—a blend of oils which is either mixed with oil colours or painted over with them, to create a transparent coloured glaze with a waxy consistency. Because of its transparency, scumble glaze allows for a very subtle colour effect—rather like a stained-glass window, where you can see the colour of the glass while the background colour is still evident. If, for example, you apply red oil paint to a scumble-glazed white surface, you can see the red clearly, but the white shows through. If you change the base colour, you will change the effect. The glaze can be thinned with white spirit to obtain the consistency you prefer.

One word of warning—never leave rags soaked in scumble glaze bunched up when not in use. The chemical reaction is such that they can burst into flames. Leave rags laid out flat overnight so that the glaze will evaporate.

Preparation
The surface on which you are going to paint has to be properly prepared before you begin to decorate it (see following steps). The glaze will adhere to French polish and various other finishes, but if you cannot identify the finish, you should test that the surface is suitable. Apply scumble glaze to a hidden area, and leave to dry. Stick down some masking tape, and pull it off. If the glaze remains on the surface, you can go ahead. If the glaze is lifted with the tape, the surface finish will need to be removed by carefully rubbing down with water-soaked wet and dry paper, before you are ready to begin applying an eggshell base colour.

Types of marbling

Payne's grey paint and glaze, stippled with a synthetic sponge.

Payne's grey and Venetian red, stippled then rag-rolled.

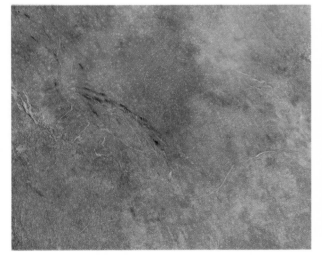

The table marbled in the steps, has a Venetian red glaze, with Payne's grey added in patches and veins.

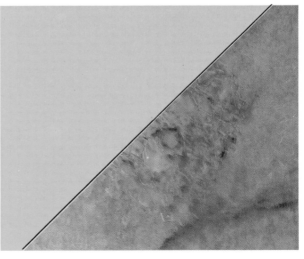

The marbling technique using Payne's grey and Venetian red, but with a cinnamon base colour.

How to prepare the surface

How you prepare the surface for marbling will depend upon its state, and what finish it has. There are two basic rules: it must be absolutely smooth, and it must be able to 'take' the glaze—that is, the glaze must adhere to it.

Bare wood must be sealed with a coat of primer/sealer, then filled with an oil-based grain filler (see page 31 for grain filling), if necessary. Sand the surface with water-soaked wet and dry paper on a sanding block, and paint with at least two coats of eggshell paint—rub back gently with wet and dry between coats, and after final coat. Allow to dry thoroughly before applying glaze.

If the surface is painted, or has some other sort of finish, but is scratched (as was the table), rub down with wet and dry until it feels silky smooth, fill any holes and sand smooth. Apply at least two coats of eggshell paint, and rub lightly with water-soaked wet and dry.

Above: This old table had been French polished—a surface which will accept scumble glaze. However, the surface was badly scratched, and the veneer chipped, so it needed sound and time consuming preparation.

WHAT YOU NEED
Wet and dry paper, Water, Sanding block
Rubber gloves
Soap or washing-up liquid
White spirit, Cloth
Fine-grade glass paper
Proprietary filler, Spatula
Paint brush, Primer (if necessary)
Eggshell paint (colour of your choice)

1 Soak wet and dry paper in water, wrap it round a sanding block, and rub surface until it feels silky smooth. It is helpful to soap the surface first, with soap or washing-up liquid.

2 Fill any holes with proprietary filler. Allow to dry, then sand smooth with fine-grade glass paper, followed by wet and dry. Wipe over the entire surface with white spirit.

3 Once the white spirit has evaporated, apply a coat of oil-based eggshell paint. Allow to dry, rub back with wet and dry paper, apply a second coat and allow to dry.

How to marble

The following steps show you how to use traditional techniques of stippling, rag-rolling and veining to create a unique decorative effect.

Before you begin, open the windows to ensure good ventilation. Experiment with the various techniques on sample boards until you get the feel of the medium, and discover the effects you particularly like. Do not worry if things go wrong. Any effect that you do not like can be 'banged out' with the end of a brush, or a sponge, then reworked.

Use the stippling and rag-rolling techniques in any order, and in whichever areas you want, using your eye to determine if and when to add more colour, and how to distribute the patterns.

WHAT YOU NEED
Scumble glaze, White spirit
Palette knife (optional)
Board for mixing colours
Artist's oil colour paints
Synthetic sponge, Rags, Feathers (with and/or without a serrated edge)
Old brush for applying glaze and colour
Hog's hair softening brush
Hog's hair brush for varnishing
Silk and gloss polyurethane varnish
Grade 0000 wire wool
Wax furniture polish
Soft cloth for waxing surface at end

1 Using an old brush, apply a thin layer of scumble glaze over the entire surface. Apply glaze to sides as well as top, so that you can work on both simultaneously.

2 Dip the brush into the oil paint, and bang it down randomly all over the glazed surface. The idea is to achieve a mottled effect. The (white) base colour will glow through.

3 Use a synthetic sponge to stipple areas of the mottle surface. Dab with the sponge to soften random areas of colour—stipple as much of the surface as you like.

4 If you think that the colour looks too light at this (or any) stage, use the brush to dab on more dense areas of colour. Make colour patches flow along and over on to side edges.

41

5 To increase the variety of texture, take a bunch of rags and dab this on to the surface in random areas. As you work, judge the developing pattern and texture by eye.

6 To break up the colour even further, use the bunch of rags to rag-roll. Using both hands, press your fingers into the bunch of rags as you roll it randomly across the surface.

7 You may like to add another colour. If so, take a clean brush, and apply second colour in random patches—making them as large or as small as you like.

8 Bang out the second colour by pounding it with a sponge—or use a sponge and bunch of rags at the same time, bouncing them on to the surface to merge the colours.

9 When you are happy with the pattern and texture, use a hog's hair softening brush to soften and merge the colours, and smooth the surface. Flick the brush gently over surface.

10 To add the painted veins, dip the side of a feather into paint, angle it at 45 degrees, and drag it gently across surface in lines to mimic the veins found in real marble.

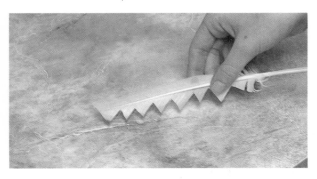

11 Soften the painted veins with the softening brush as in Step 9, flicking it gently over the surface in random directions until you are happy with the result.

12 You can also make the veins by taking off colour. Dip the serrated edge of a feather into white spirit, and drag it lightly across the surface to create (in this case) fine white veins.

13 To increase the mottled effect, spatter random patches with white spirit. Dip a brush in white spirit, and bang it across the handle of another brush.

14 Once you are happy with the final effect, allow to dry thoroughly, then varnish—using a good quality brush—with one coat of gloss, and two coats of satin varnish

Once the paint is completely dry you should give it three coats of varnish—one of gloss, two of satin. Rub back very gently with water-soaked wet-and-dry between coats and after the final coat.

CHAPTER 2

Painting & Papering

Every householder knows what quick and easy results can be achieved by giving a room a new coat of paint or a change of wallpaper. In this chapter we start by going back to basics with a section on surface preparation—washing down the walls, stripping paint and paper, repairing defects such as mould, damp, holes and cracks—and applying emulsion paint. Next, the techniques of creating pretty painted borders on a plain wall or ceiling are explored—make your own original pattern or follow our striking geometric design. Stencilling is another way to brighten up dull surfaces; we show you how to cut the boards and apply the paint for the best results. The chapter closes with a section on techniques for hanging many of the different types of wall coverings that are on the market today.

Surface preparation and emulsion painting

Although you may be tempted to cut corners at this stage, don't! It is simply not worth it, as the results will be disappointing and the money spent on decorating materials wasted.

Starting work

Preparatory work is messy, so begin by clearing out as much furniture from the room you are decorating as possible. Move the rest into the middle of the room and cover it and the floor with polythene sheets or dustsheets—old, worn-out bed linen is ideal.

The next job is to identify the surface to be cleaned or stripped. This is important since different surfaces need different treatment; for example, gloss paint and distemper. Paint should be thoroughly cleaned (though it is sometimes best to strip it completely) while wall coverings should be removed. A new wall covering will probably not adhere to an old one. The surface must then be made good by dealing with defects like small holes, cracks, mould growth or crumbling plaster. When these repairs are complete, and the surface is thoroughly clean and dry, the paint and new wall covering can be applied.

Preparing painted surfaces

First, vacuum-clean the junction between the ceiling and

A change of paint can make a dramatic difference to a room. Use two coats of emulsion paint as a minimum for a professional-looking finish

walls to remove cobwebs and dust, then wash down all of the surfaces with mild detergent and warm water. Neglected walls will need a stronger cleaner like sugar soap, which is a mild abrasive, dissolved in warm water.

Textured paints can be stripped, if wished, with a proprietary textured-paint remover—which is toxic and needs to be handled with care.

Old distemper must be removed altogether by washing down the surface repeatedly with frequent changes of water or it can be sealed with waterproof sealer, before redecorating. If this is not done, you will find that the new surface will not adhere to the old.

Removing wallpaper

Some wallpapers are easy to remove; others, particularly when there are several layers or if they have been coated with paint, can prove more difficult. Light-weight wall coverings that have been recently hung (say within the last two years), will strip off easily, needing only hot water and a thorough soaking.

If you are tackling several layers of heavier, painted papers (lining papers and embossed papers), these may prove extremely difficult to remove. Here, a proprietary

wallpaper stripper is required. Heavier, embossed papers covered with paint may need scoring with a wire brush first, to allow the stripper solution to penetrate through to the paste beneath.

If none of these methods remove stubborn wall coverings —if there is a build-up of wallpaper and paint or if there is a large amount of stripping needed—then steam strippers are recommended. These need to be handled with care: if the pad is held too closely and too long near the walls, it can bring away not only the paper but weak plaster, although this is more likely to happen in old houses where the plaster has been allowed to deteriorate.

Never try to use a steam stripper on ceilings: the hose is too short and it can be danger-

ous working overhead with a steam pad.

Hire the electrically operated steam strippers only from a hire shop which supplies full instructions and is able to answer individual questions expertly. Fill up the tank with water, wait for the steam to build up then hold the pad near the wall only until the paper begins to absorb the steam. Do a test first to see how long you need to keep the pad near the wall.

Repair work

Once the walls are stripped, there is often a defective surface to be made good before a top finish can be applied, and it is worth spending time on this. The source and cause of defects like mould and damp must be located and treated.

Cleaning painted surfaces

Most surfaces require only a light clean or sponge. If they have been neglected, however, they need an abrasive cleaner such as sugar soap mixed with warm water, to degrease the surface, or the new paint will

not adhere. Gloss-painted surfaces should be keyed, that is slightly roughened with coarse sandpaper. This helps the next surface covering to adhere. If you wish, gloss paint can be stripped.

WHAT YOU NEED
Vacuum cleaner,
Sponge
Coarse sandpaper
Gloves, Sugar soap

1 Thoroughly clean surfaces with sugar soap solution. Use a sponge and work upwards. Rinse and dry.

2 Roughen gloss-painted surfaces by lightly sanding with medium sandpaper to provide a good key.

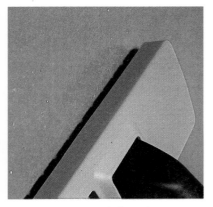

3 Using a soft brush attachment on the vacuum cleaner, carefully vacuum off all dust created by sanding.

Preparing textured surfaces

The surface may have been treated with textured paints to disguise defective plastering. This can be stripped off, if wished, with proprietary textured-paint remover. It is lengthy and messy work, which has to be followed by careful renovation of the walls, where necessary. Alternatively, vacuum the surface, then wash down. Allow to dry before repainting.

WHAT YOU NEED
Gloves and overalls
Wide stripping knife
Textured-paint remover

1 Vacuum textured paints, then wash down as for gloss paint or strip off. Wear protective gloves and clothing, apply remover with a brush and leave for one hour.

2 When paint begins to soften and bubble, strip it off with a wide scraper, taking great care not to damage the wall. Thoroughly wash down surface with cold water. Leave to dry.

Stripping vinyl wall coverings

Many vinyl wall coverings have backing papers which will stay fixed to the wall when the top coating is pulled away. Start at a corner of the ceiling and use a knife to ease open a seam. When the top coat has been stripped and any loose backing paper repaired, this can be used as a surface (if the paper is in good condition) for new paper. However, if you are painting the wall, remove the backing.

WHAT YOU NEED
Blunt knife
Fine sandpaper
Wallpaper brush
Latex adhesive

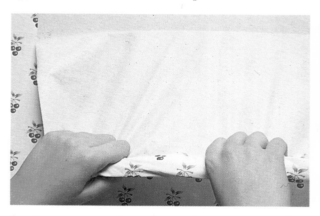

1 Locate a starting edge at the seams, ease it away from the wall and pull off the whole length, working from the top downwards. It should come away quite easily

2 Sandpaper back any odd nicks, stick down any loose seams with latex adhesive applied on a brush or thin spatula, and brush down the backing paper to remove dust.

Stripping easily removed wallpaper

A recently hung light-weight paper will usually strip off easily. First of all try pulling it away from the wall. Find a starting point at a seam edge with a blunt knife or the corner of a scraper. If this does not prove successful, then all that is usually needed is a thorough soaking with hot water. To make the stripping easier, be sure to allow plenty of time for the water to soak into the paper.

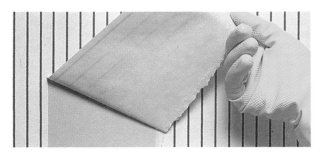

1 With a sponge, generously soak the walls and ceiling with hot water. Leave for one hour to give the water an opportunity of soaking through to the paste beneath.

2 Once the paper is soaked it should lift away from the walls easily. Slide the stripping knife under the paper at a seam edge. The paper should come away in wide strips.

Stripping stubborn wallpaper

Some old wallpapers are more difficult to remove. They may have been in place for many years and in some cases, pasted on top of the others. These papers may respond well to treatment with a solution of proprietary wallpaper stripper.

Other walls may respond better to treatment with a steam stripper—be sure to follow the hire company's instructions.

1 Test on a small hidden area to make sure the steam has built up sufficiently. When it has, hold pad to wall. Start with about 15 seconds, work up to one minute, if necessary.

2 Move the stripper away from the wall and place it on its side out of harm's way. It will drip, so protect the floor with polythene sheeting. Peel off the paper with a scraper.

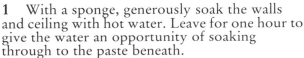

Filling cracks and holes

Small cracks and holes, often caused by shelving, pictures, mirrors and other objects should always be thoroughly cleaned out so that the filler used will bond well. Fill in the cracks and holes with a cellulose filler, allow this to harden, then smooth down with sandpaper until the filler is flush with the wall.

As cellulose filler is expensive, use plaster rather than filler for large holes, after part-filling the hole with paper.

For still further economy, fill large holes with a four to one mixture of sand and cement, then finish with a layer of plaster.

Cellulose filler can be tinted by mixing it with emulsion paint to match the surrounding area.

> ## WHAT YOU NEED
> Old knife, Filling knife,
> Cellulose filler
> Small brush, Sandpaper

1 Rake out any dust and lumps of broken plaster with a knife and cut back any crumbling or loose plaster surrounding the hole to give a firm edge for the new filling.

2 Make sure that the hole is completely clear of any loose pieces, then carefully dust down surrounding cracks with a wire brush to remove any remaining loose material.

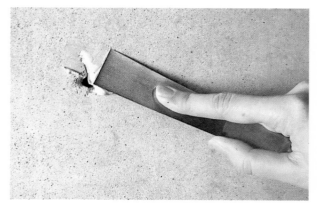

3 Fill with cellulose filler, pressing it in well, and leaving it just proud of surface. Dampen deep holes with a wet brush and fill in layers, allowing each to harden before adding next.

4 When the last layer of filler is completely hard, carefully sand down so that it is level with the surrounding edges. Finish by brushing away all dust.

Making crumbling plaster good

Crumbling plaster is often caused by damp and it is vital that the cause of the damp is located and dealt with before redecorating begins otherwise the results will be sadly short-lived. All damaged plaster should be removed and the surrounding plaster should be thoroughly dry.

WHAT YOU NEED
Stabilizing primer
Wire brush
Paint brush

1 Let plaster dry out completely—use a hair-dryer to speed up process. Remove damaged plaster with wire brush until dry edge is found. Fill as for cracks and holes.

2 Where large patches of flaking plaster have been repaired, brush on a stabilizing primer over these areas to seal the surface ready for its new coat. Allow primer to dry.

Treating mould

Caused by damp or condensation, mould looks like black spotting on the wall. It attacks the wallpaper paste, breaking it down. The paste crystallizes and the paper begins to come away from the wall. Treat affected areas with bleach.

WHAT YOU NEED
Household bleach,
Bucket
Brush, Mild detergent,
Sponge

1 Mix one part household bleach to 16 parts water, and liberally brush on to the affected area. Do not skimp on this part of the treatment. Leave the bleach on for four hours.

2 Make up a solution of warm water and washing-up liquid to wash off mould. Rinse down with clean water. Apply a second bleach solution; leave to dry for 72 hours.

Preparing distempered surfaces

Distemper is an old water-based paint, which will flake off if you try to paint on top of it. To identify it, place a small piece of sticky tape on the wall. If the tape brings the paint layer with it when removed, it is probably distemper and will need to be removed.

1 Dip sponge in the water, squeeze out excess, then wash down wall (or ceiling). Do this repeatedly, changing the water each time it becomes cloudy with distemper.

2 When as much as possible has been removed, paint the wall with stabilizing solution to seal in any remaining distemper. Allow to dry before applying new finish.

Painting the walls

When all surfaces are flat, smooth and clean, they are ready for either wallpapering or for a coat of emulsion paint or gloss painting. There are various types of emulsion suitable for ceilings and walls—some give a flat finish known as matt, others produce a silky look known as silk or sheen. The latter gives an attractive, hard-wearing finish but highlights any slight undulation on the walls where the light falls on them.

Choose a warm, dry day for painting if possible, as a damp atmosphere can slow down the drying process. Ventilate the room well so that paint smells will be dispersed quickly and lay down protective floor coverings.

Starting the job
Ceilings should be tackled first and then walls. When painting walls, always start from the window and work outwards from either side. For ceilings, work from the window wall across to the opposite side of the room. If there is more than one window in the room, begin at the window with most light. Strong light will show any irregularities. Work in manageable strips across the ceiling; on walls start at the top and work down.

Always read the instructions on the tin before making a start and allow plenty of time to tackle a complete wall or ceiling in one go. If you have to stop half-way through, you will have an unsightly 'tide-mark' where you left off.

There is a wide range of tools available for applying emulsion paint. Brushes give good results but rollers tend to be less messy and much quicker and are especially suitable for covering large areas. Paint pads are useful for awkward places, for example round light switches or power points or for painting next to skirting boards and door frames. Experiment with all these tools to find those that best suit your needs.

Always wash out tools in warm detergent and water solution as soon as you finish painting. Dried paint is very difficult to remove and, if left, will shorten the life of your equipment.

How to work out your quantities

One litre of matt emulsion will cover approximately 10 sq metres (on a standard 198cm-high wall it will cover 550cm); a silk sheen finish will cover about 9 sq metres. Check on the paint tin as covering capacity varies from one brand to another. Also bear in mind that a roller will use more emulsion paint than a brush.

Two coats of emulsion paint are usually recommended as a minimum but if painting a light colour over a darker one, expect to apply more coats for good covering power. Also, if the walls are quite porous—for example, if you are painting on bare or new plaster—a base coat of emulsion thinned with a little clean water should be applied to prime the surface. When applying subsequent coats, do not dilute the paint to make it go further. This is a false economy as the thinner the paint, the more coats you need to apply for a good result.

How to use emulsion paint

When working on ceilings, make a platform with two stepladders and a plank. Always work on clean surfaces. Use paint pads or narrow brushes for difficult areas. At the end of each day's work, wash out roller head, brushes or pads in warm detergent solution.

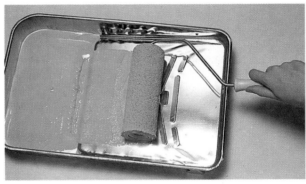

1 Decant some of the emulsion into a paint roller tray. Load the roller with paint by rolling it back and forth. Remove excess by running the roller up the slope of the tray.

2 Work in half-metre strips from the window. Use alternating diagonal strokes to avoid leaving obvious overlap marks; finish each section by lifting upwards to prevent ridges.

3 Use a 2.5cm-wide brush, edge on, to paint up to window reveal and junction of ceiling and wall. Do not use a roller here, as it will smudge and not cover satisfactorily.

4 When covering difficult areas, such as round light switches or at edges of skirtings, use either a paint pad or a narrow brush, taking care not to overload with emulsion.

Simple painted borders

Painted borders can create a variety of effects. They can change the apparent shape and proportions of a room: high ceilings, for example, can be effectively 'lowered' if ceiling and walls about 30cm down are painted in a deep colour with a contrasting border below. If your wall is long and low, change the proportions with vertical borders along the wall edges, and a horizontal border across the top. Or use a border as a decorative feature in its own right.

Clean-edged lines and an imaginative use of colour are the keys to the success of any striped border. The range of effects is endless, yet it relies on one easy technique—that of painting between lines of masking tape.

The base surface
Painted plaster walls, or flat wooden panels such as doors, are the easiest surfaces on which to paint borders. When painting on wood, you will probably want to use gloss paints. Vinyl silk (rather than matt) is the best type of paint for the background on the walls, since it is less likely to come away when masking tape is removed. But don't worry if the wall has a matt finish—just be more careful when pulling off tape.

Walls lined with plain or very lightly textured paper are also quite suitable, as long as

No special skill or extra-steady hand is needed to paint a simple border.

care is taken. Heavily textured wallpapers, such as some varieties of woodchip, are difficult to paint well, since the uneven, raised surface cannot be masked properly and may even pull away when the tape is removed. In this case, paint the stripes directly on to lining paper, cut them to size and paste on to the wall for a similar effect.

You may feel wary of attempting your first border in your living room or dining room. If so, why not try a bathroom border? Use the simple border on the opposite page, or the more adventurous, zigzag pattern on page 60. An actual-size pattern of the zigzag motif appears on page 61, accompanied by instructions for making the necessary templates. Although this design looks more complicated, it is achieved simply with masking tape.

Design and colour
The colours of the border should complement the colour of the wall, door or panel which you are painting. Try to decide, as far as possible, the colours which you want to overlay. Then paint strips of leftover wallpaper using leftover emulsion, or buy miniature tester pots to paint a small sample. Stick or pin the sample to the wall for a few days to help you decide exactly the effect you want to create. Alternatively, you could buy a few sheets of coloured paper—or paint white paper—to try out your proposed scheme. By cutting the painted wallpaper or coloured paper into strips of different widths, and placing the strips in different positions, you can decide exactly what looks best—before any paint has touched the wall!

How to paint a simple, striped border

WHAT YOU NEED
Emulsion paints—colours of your choice for the border
Leftover paint for retouching
Lengths of old wallpaper, or coloured paper
Stiff card for templates

Masking tape
Steel ruler
Spirit level (optional, but very useful)
Paint brushes (including one artist's water-colour brush for any retouching work)

How to work out your quantities
See page 53 for covering rate of emulsion paints. If there is enough left, and you like the colour, use any leftovers that you have saved from a previous painting job.

1 Try out proposed design by cutting pieces of painted wallpaper or coloured strips of paper, and positioning them against wall. When satisfied, start on the wall itself.

2 Using the top of skirting board (or wall corner, or ceiling line) as base level, mark position of outer stripe's edge. Then draw a line between marked points.

3 Stick masking tape along outer edge of marked line. Cut a card template the same depth as proposed stripe; rest it on the tape, then mark along the stripe's inner edge.

4 Mask the inner edge with tape. Press tape edges down firmly, to prevent paint seeping underneath. Paint in between the masked edges, using long, even strokes.

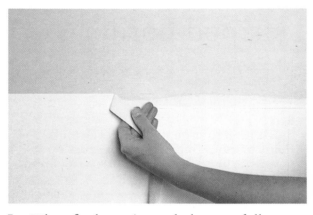

5 When final coat is touch dry, carefully peel away the masking tape. Pull the masking tape down and back at the same time. Touch up any runs by hand.

6 Allow first stripe to dry for three days before overpainting any other stripes. Then mask and paint as before. Leave paint until touch dry, and repeat Step 5.

Ideas for using borders

The border technique does not have to be limited to painting main wall areas. There are numerous ways in which you can extend the effect—to accentuate features such as pictures or mirrors, or to decorate your furnishing fabrics. To achieve an integrated look, you could extend a painted border around the room, following the lines of doors and windows. Or create an interesting and welcoming effect in a hall using a wide border to lead the eye towards and up the stairs.

Try out different ideas—like matching the pattern, but varying the colour combinations on different objects. Alternatively, you could create a simplified version of a wall border on your furnishing. For example, if you painted the zigzag border on page 60 above the bath, you could make matching towels, perhaps by picking up one or two colours from the wall border, and sewing strips of colour-fast ribbon along the towels' edges. And as long as the effect is not too overpowering for your particular bathroom, you could even repeat the zigzag motif on the side of the bath itself.

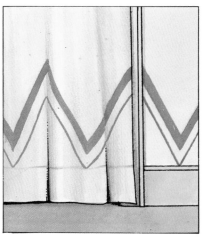

Top left: Self-adhesive vinyl borders along the edges of kitchen cupboards can be used to achieve an original look on mass-produced furniture.

Above: Painted stripes on walls or tables can be echoed on furnishing accessories.

Bottom left: Brighten up the corners of the ceiling by painting a stepped border on the wall, echoed by a simpler border on the ceiling itself. Or add interest to the wall features by surrounding them with a striped border.

Left: The complementary colours of the striped mirror border create the effect of a bright frame.

How to paint a geometric border

WHAT YOU NEED
Pencil, Ruler
Spirit level (optional, but a good idea)
Stiff card and a set-square for making templates
13mm-wide masking tape
Artist's water-colour brushes (No. 4)
Scissors, Sharp craft knife, Rubber
Emulsion paint in various colours
Paper (if you are making up your own design—or use actual-size pattern on page 61)

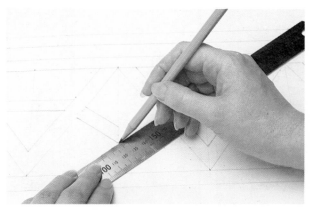

1 For design above, use pattern on page 61, but if designing your own motif, draw it to full size on paper. Measure, mark and mask baseline as in Steps 2 and 3, pages 55–6.

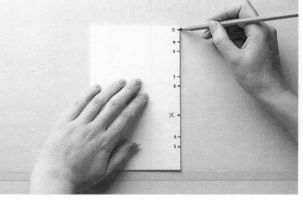

2 Make a card template (see page 60), hold it above base tape. Make pencil marks on wall against all but line marked X. Move template along, and repeat.

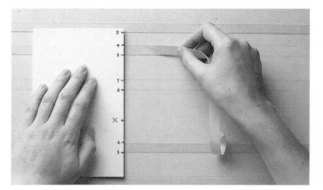

3 Join up marks horizontally, and stick strips of masking tape between lines 1 and 2, 3 and 4, and above line 5. Use template to check that the tapes are in correct position.

4 Make a template, 11cm deep and marked top to bottom at 7cm intervals. Starting at corner, use template to mark inner two tapes at 7cm intervals. Join marks vertically.

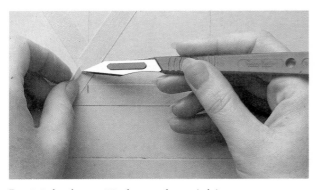 

5 Make large V-shapes by sticking tapes diagonally between alternate upper and lower 7cm marks. The tape's *lower* edge should touch marks. Trim to point with knife.

6 Mask between V-shapes (*not* inverted Vs), by sticking tape between lines 6 and 7. Check with template to ensure correct positioning, and trim overlaps with scissors.

 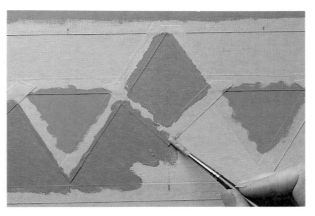

7 Hold template against vertical lines between inverted Vs and mark against point X. Use tape to form small Vs, positioning lower edges between points 6 and X. Trim.

8 Once all the tapes are in position, smooth down along edges, and paint in appropriate colours. Brush *away* from tape edges, to prevent paint from getting underneath.

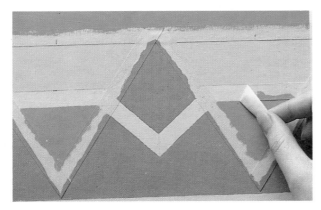 

9 Leave until touch-dry, then remove tapes carefully—pulling off overlapping pieces first. Leave to dry completely, then remove any pencil marks with a rubber.

The most rewarding moment of all is when you remove the final strip of tape to reveal the finished border.

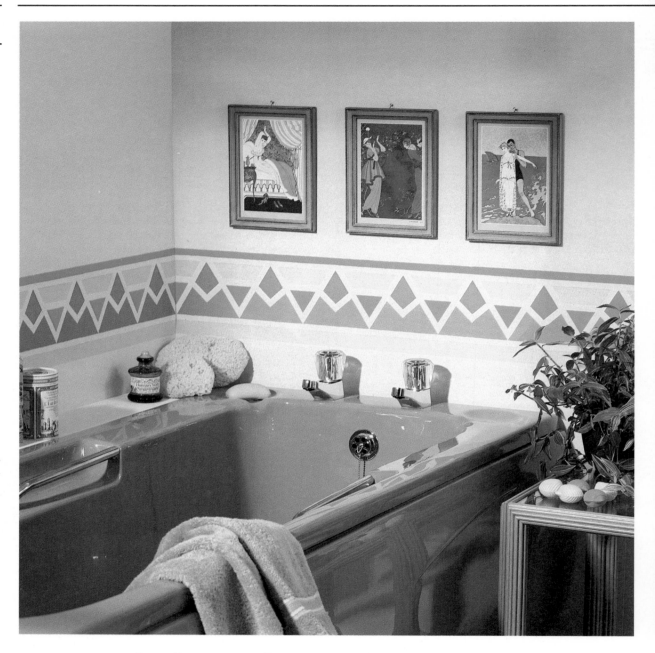

How to make the templates

To make the process as easy as possible, it is advisable to make two templates. The first is made by laying a card template, 18cm by 11cm, on the pattern opposite and marking where the upper and lower edges of the horizontal strips of tape are to be positioned. First, lay the card on top of the lowest tape—mark and number as shown above (the tape between points 6 and 7 are the final vertical strips to be applied). Then, move template along, and align it with the vertical line running down between the inverted V-shapes, and mark the card with an X at the point where it touches the lower point of the small V-shape.

To make the second template, simply cut a rectangular piece of card, 11cm deep and about 42cm long and mark from top to bottom edges at 7cm intervals along its length.

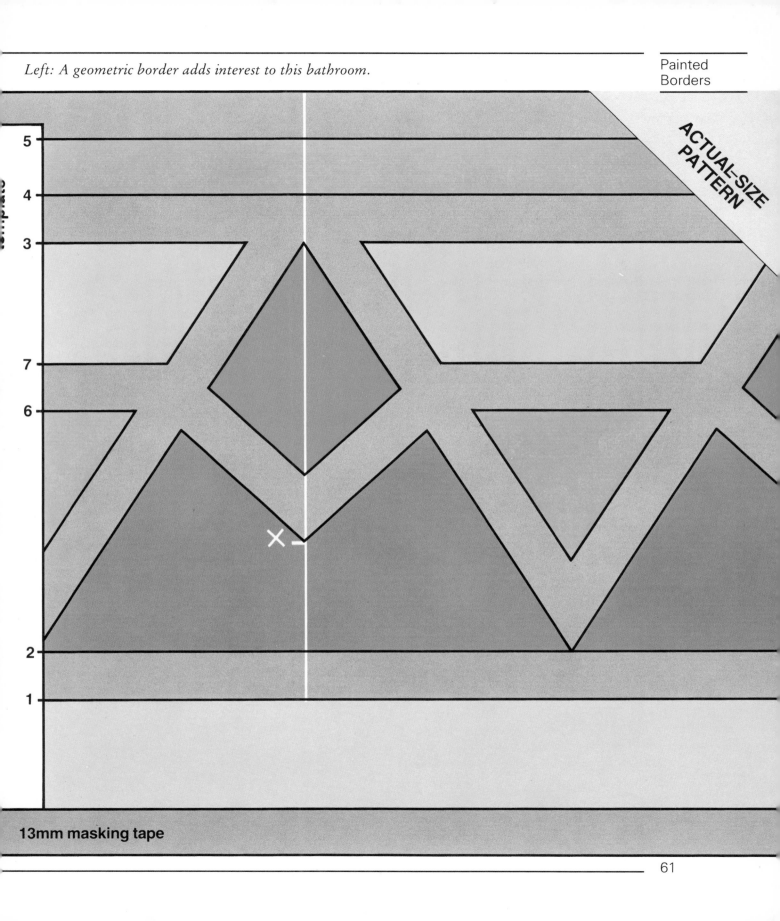

Left: A geometric border adds interest to this bathroom.

ACTUAL-SIZE
PATTERN

5

4

3

Template

7

6

2

1

× −

13mm masking tape

Using stencils

Stencilling was originally used to decorate walls before wallpaper became cheap enough for everyone to buy. Today this technique can be used not only to colour co-ordinate any room in the home, but also to decorate pieces of furniture or add interest to plain walls or floorboards. Any surface that can be painted can be stencilled, which means that the possibilities for decoration are almost limitless.

Decorative styles can vary from the brightest of primary colours to subtle pastel tones that blend sympathetically with the surrounding furnishings.

Materials

Although there is a wide range of ready-cut stencils on sale in art shops, don't think only in terms of these. You can make your own stencils by taking the pattern from a piece of furnishing fabric or wallpaper, trace a motif from a book or magazine photograph or, in a child's bedroom, base the design on favourite cartoon character or animal.

If you do decide to cut your own stencil, make sure that you use an extremely sharp craft knife. Either sharpen or replace the blade before each session for best results, as it is important to cut a very clean edge on the stencil and a knife that is too blunt will tear the stencil as you cut.

Buy special oiled stencil board which can be used again if cleaned with solvent. It is best not to use cardboard since the fibres make it difficult to achieve a firm edge when cutting a stencil; in turn this means that the edges of the painted stencil will look fuzzy.

You can use a variety of paints, but they must be fairly thick to avoid running. Artist's acrylic paints (sold in art shops) are particularly good for stencilling on walls, although you could use leftover pots of oil-based paints or small trial-size pots of emulsion. Experiment with different types of paint to find out which works best on your surface. Although you can buy special stencil brushes, a small piece of sponge is quite adequate.

Preparation

Whichever surface you are stencilling, you must make sure that it is clean and sound. Always test emulsioned walls before you begin; fix a piece of adhesive tape to the wall and gently pull it off. If the tape brings the paint with it, you will need to rub back any flaking paint and apply a new coat before stencilling. Otherwise walls can simply be washed down with a sugar-soap solution to prepare them for stencilling.

If you are stencilling wooden furniture, you can also use a sugar-soap solution if the finish is sound; if it is not, you will need to fill any gaps or chips with a wood stopping—see page 34 for more details. If you are adding a new finish to the wood, apply three base coats, lightly sanding in between, then do a final wipe-down with a clean cloth dampened with white spirit

Always practise on a piece of hardboard before stencilling your surface. You may change your mind about the paint colours or the stencil motif, and practising beforehand will avoid having to repaint the surface.

The flower pattern on the curtains was the inspiration for the motif on the stencilled border.

How to make your pattern

When you first make your own stencil, don't be too ambitious—choose a well defined shape that can be easily adapted either as a single motif or repeated as a border.

If you are tracing off a design from fabric, make sure the fabric is held rigid—pin it out on stiff card—and use ordinary tracing paper to trace off the design.

If you are stencilling a border, it is advisable to trace a number of individual motifs from a design, then to move them round until you achieve an interesting continuous pattern.

When you have worked out your design, transfer it on to a piece of oiled stencil card, using a piece of carbon paper in between the tracing and board to give a strong outline. Fix the tracing into position with small pieces of sticky tape at each corner, then use a ball-point pen to retrace the design, pressing down firmly so that it is transferred to the stencil board.

WHAT YOU NEED
Fabric, wallpaper or photograph
Soft pencil, Tracing paper
Biro, Sticky tape
Oiled stencil board or sheets of acetate
Scissors, Carbon paper

1 Place fabric or other motif on a flat surface, and use a soft pencil to trace off the sections you want to use. If necessary, fix the fabric down with tape to prevent it slipping.

2 Once you have traced off a number of different motifs from the fabric, cut the tracing paper so that you can move the motifs around until you like the arrangement.

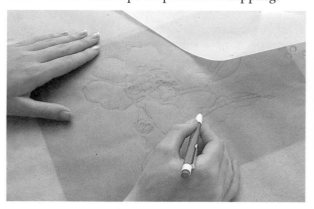

3 Transfer your tracing to the stencil board by placing carbon paper between and use a ball-point pen to retrace the outlines. Hold the tracing in position with sticky tape.

4 At this stage simplify the pattern if necessary, omitting some of the finer details that could be painted in when the main stencilling has been completed.

How to cut the stencil

To protect the surface you are cutting on, use a piece of smooth plywood or chipboard as the knife needs to be used firmly on the stencil board. If you are going to do a lot of stencilling, you can buy special cutting boards from art shops.

Plenty of patience is needed meticulously to cut round the traced outlines, taking particular care when you come to sections or 'bridges' (which can be quite narrow) separating one area from another.

Make sure the blade is very sharp so that you can achieve a very clean edge on the stencil —a ragged one will produce uneven finishes when the paint has been applied. Try to cut

with the blade at right angles to the board.

If you make a mistake when cutting the stencil, you can repair the damage by using small pieces of sticky tape to stick the pieces together on the underside. Make sure the tape does not overlap on to the edges of the stencil. Cut the very large areas last as the stencil weakens as the cutting-out proceeds.

WHAT YOU NEED
Strong cutting board
Very sharp craft knife
Stencilled design

1 Starting with the smaller areas, cut out the board, applying firm pressure on the knife to produce a clean edge. If it helps, stand rather than sit at the cutting board.

2 To achieve a clean edge when cutting out curves, gradually move the stencil round rather than the knife itself. Any slight imperfections can be lightly sanded.

Stencilling method 1

Before you start to paint on the design with the stencil, make sure the surface is sound. If not, carry out the necessary preparation work, recoat the surface and leave it to dry. You can use a variety of different paints on the surface, but they need to be fairly thick to prevent seepage under the edges of the stencil. Artist's acrylic paints thinned down, will provide good, strong colours and dry quickly, but you can also use emulsion paints and oil-based paints, like glosses and lacquers. Signwriter's enamels are often used because they dry extremely quickly, but they can be difficult to buy unless you have a specialist paint supplier nearby. If necessary,

mix the paints to achieve the desired shades but try them out first.

WHAT YOU NEED
Selection of acrylic or other paints
Palette knife
Old plate
Stencil brush or piece of sponge
Artist's paint brush
Masking tape

1 Use small pots of paint to obtain a range of different colours by mixing them up on an old plate or piece of card. Experiment to achieve the correct creamy consistency.

2 Always test wall finish first by applying a small piece of sticky tape. If it pulls off paint, rub down and repaint. Allow to dry thoroughly before stencilling.

3 Make sure the stencil is correctly aligned, if necessary using a rigid rule and spirit level. Then fix into position using pieces of sticky tape at each corner.

4 Using a virtually dry stencil brush or sponge, 'pounce'—dab on paint with brush vertical—the areas, making sure the paint covers well. If the area is very small, brush or wipe across.

5 Acrylic paints dry very quickly, allowing you to pull away the stencil easily. When using emulsion, you must check it is beginning to dry first.

6 It is easier to fill in tiny details after the stencil has been removed. Use a fine artist's brush to give the lightest finishing touches to the stencil.

Stencilling method 2

Apart from using a single stencil to produce interesting patterns and designs, you can also go a step further and overlap the first stencil with a second to bring detail to the design. This can be filled in with either a complementary shade or a contrast and will give the design a totally different look, quite unlike the broken effect of an ordinary stencil.

Cut out two pieces of stencil board the same size, transfer the body of your design on to one piece of stencil, place the second piece over the top, then transfer the detail by using a ball-point pen as on page 64. Cut out each stencil (see page 65), then cut notches through both pieces to make sure the designs are correctly aligned.

When working on wood as shown here, you must also clean down the surface with sugar soap and repaint where necessary. Allow the new paint to dry thoroughly. Any oil-based paints are ideal for wood, and you can use leftover pots of gloss paint or use tiny pots of enamel.

WHAT YOU NEED
**Scissors, Stencil board, Tracing paper
Pieces of foam rubber, Old plate
Paints, Polyurethane varnish
Paintbrush**

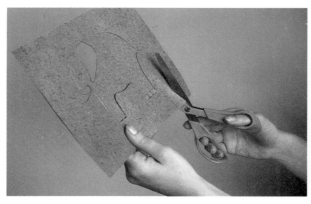

1 Transfer main part of design to one board and cut out (see page 65). Transfer and cut details on second board. Using sharp scissors, trim excess board.

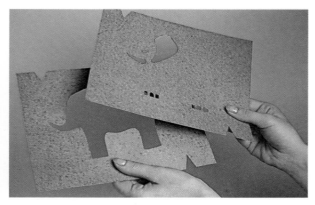

2 Once boards are cut, make sure that the details are correctly aligned to main design by cutting matching notches through boards at the same time.

3 Cut up small pieces of foam rubber and use them to dab the paint on to the main outline. Use one end of the foam, then let it dry and use the other end.

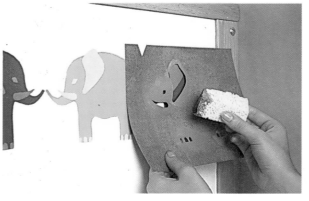

4 Once the main outlines have been painted in and are completely dry, use contrast colours to fill in the details. Make sure the foam is not overloaded with paint.

5 Often when the design has been stencilled, there are tiny missed or ragged edges. Use a fine artist's brush to touch in, taking care not to overload the brush with paint.

6 For extra toughness, it is best to protect the pattern by using a polyurethane varnish. Use a clean brush to coat each motif lightly, and leave to dry.

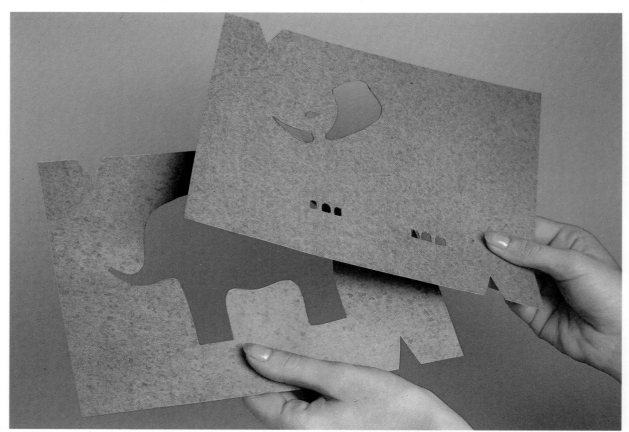

When you are using a stencil to give a main outline which will be filled in, and a second to pick out detail, like the elephant's ears, tusk feet and eyes, you will need to make sure that the details are correctly aligned with the main sections. By cutting notches through both stencils at the same time, this will ensure exact matching when using this stencilling method. Always use lead-free paint when stencilling on children's furniture.

Where to stencil

There is almost no limit to the ways in which stencils can enhance and personalize your home, since any surface that can be painted can be stencilled. Wood is perhaps the most obvious surface to use, but metals and plastics can equally well be decorated with this technique. Take care, however, to use the correct paint so that the stencilled motif will adhere permanently to the chosen surface, even in humid rooms such as the kitchen or bathroom.

Use emulsion paint to work a simple repeat design on a contrast-colour border at dado height.

Acrylic paint can be used to work a simple border at picture rail height. Repeat the design elsewhere in the room.

Use coloured interior varnish to stencil sealed wooden floorboards and bath panel. Clear varnish to protect.

Hanging wall coverings

Nowadays the range of wall coverings available is so comprehensive that there is something to suit all tastes, budgets and decorating abilities. Choose from coated papers, tough vinyls or natural materials such as wool, silk and cork. Some papers are pasted in the traditional way with brush and bucket, others are ready-pasted, needing only a soak in a water trough to activate the adhesive, and there are polythene-foam wall coverings that are stuck to a previously pasted wall.

If possible, for a first attempt at decorating, choose a small room to work on, free of awkwardly shaped doors and windows, and avoid cheap wallpapers—they are likely to tear easily when wet. When buying, check the number on the label for each roll to make sure that all the rolls are from the same batch—this will avoid colour variations.

Choosing equipment

Plumb line

A plumb line is used to find the exact vertical line by which to position the first length of wall covering. This is necessary since walls are rarely straight and so cannot be used as a guide. Buy a plumb line from a DIY shop or make your own using a piece of string long enough to reach from the ceiling to just above the skirting board and a small, heavy object. Simply tie the knob to one end of the string with a reef knot. Never be tempted to work without a plumb line—you can easily end up with gaps at the seams and patterns which do not match.

A new wall covering can transform a room in just a few hours.

Scissors

Use long, sharp scissors to cut the lengths of paper; the blades should be 28–30cm. Don't use dressmaking scissors—the paper will blunt them.

Pasting board

Folding pasting boards can be bought from DIY shops. They are usually 1.8m long and just over the width of a piece of wallpaper and they can be stacked neatly away when not needed. Alternatively, improvize with a table or board that should be at least 55cm wide and 1.8m long to provide an adequate surface for pasting. If using a table, protect the surface with a layer of plastic, as dried wallpaper adhesive is difficult to remove.

Brushes

Buy decorator's large pasting brushes and paperhanger's brushes. The latter are soft and designed to brush on the wallpaper, smoothing away the wrinkles and bubbles. All decorating brushes will last for years if washed and dried before being stored away, so buy the best you can afford and use them only for wallpapering.

Stepladder

Make a safe platform with a plank, a strong box and a stepladder from which to reach the tops of walls. Better still, use two stepladders, with a plank between them. For safety, check your stepladder each time you use it, making sure it does not rock and the steps are not slippery.

Adhesive

Different wall coverings require different adhesives. Buy the correct one for the type of wall covering being used—ask at the shop for advice if in doubt. Mix up the adhesive according to the manufacturer's instructions at least 20 minutes before it is needed. This gives it time to absorb the water and become smooth and lump free. Always make up a complete packet at a time to ensure correct consistency. Any left-over adhesive can be kept in an airtight jar and used for resticking any loose seams that may remain when decorating is finished.

WHAT YOU NEED

1 Pasting bucket
2 Protective gloves (optional)
3 Dustsheet
4 Folding pasting board
5 Sponge
6 Paperhanger's brush
7 Pasting brush
8 Plumb line
9 Chalk
10 Soft pencil, for example 2B
11 Steel tape measure
12 Seam roller
13 Large, paper-cutting scissors
14 Wall covering of your choice
15 Adhesive to suit your wall covering (if necessary)

Plus: Stepladders, plank

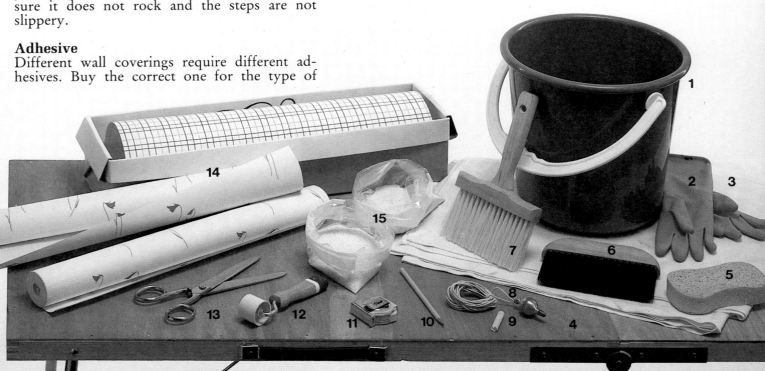

Getting started

How to work out your quantities

The chart below shows how many pre-trimmed, standard (10.05m × 53cm) rolls of wall covering you need to buy, depending on the size of your room. Measure from floor to ceiling; measure round the room. Include all doors, windows and built-in cupboards unless they are very large. Allow one roll extra for pattern matching if your wall covering has a small pattern, two if the pattern is large.

How to use this table

1 Look along top line for distance round the room. Round up to nearest measurement.
2 Look down the left-hand column for the room's height.
3 Look where **1** and **2** meet to find how many rolls you need. Allow for pattern matching as above.

Height from skirting	Measurement round walls, including doors and windows									
	8.53m	9.75m	10.97m	12.19m	13.41m	14.63m	15.83m	17.07m	18.29m	19.51m
2.13–2.29m	4	4	5	5	6	6	7	7	8	8
2.30–2.44m	4	4	5	5	6	6	7	8	8	9
2.45–2.59m	4	5	5	6	6	7	7	8	8	9
2.60–2.74m	4	5	5	6	6	7	8	8	9	9
2.75–2.90m	4	5	6	6	7	7	8	9	9	10
2.91–3.05m	5	5	6	7	7	8	9	9	10	10
3.06–3.20m	5	5	6	7	8	8	9	10	10	11

Preparing walls

Before you begin, ensure that surfaces are smooth, clean, dry and free from grease (see pages 47–52). Once the walls are prepared, it is best to 'size' them—that is to seal them and prevent the paste being absorbed too quickly. This will not only give you time to position the paper correctly on the walls, but also allow you to slide the paper up, down or sideways as required. Buy either a proprietary brand of size or use diluted wallpaper adhesive and follow the manufacturer's instructions carefully.

An expert would always advise lining the walls before papering. Lining provides a fine surface of even porosity to which the new wallpaper will stick smoothly and well. Heavy papers, particularly, may shrink on drying and when they shrink, joins open up as the paper loses its grip on the plaster—this is less likely if you line the walls. Lining paper can also disguise a poor surface and it can act as an insulating layer helping keep heat in the room.

Horizontal lining is better than vertical lining as it gives a smoother effect. If you prefer to hang the lining paper vertically, stagger the joins with those of the wallpaper to prevent the possibility of ridges forming. If wished, leave on the paper backing from previously applied vinyl wall coverings—it will act as the lining. If you do this, make sure all the seams still adhere well to the wall—repasting the seams wherever necessary—or obvious 'tramlines' may form under the new paper.

Use the chart above to work out how much lining paper you need to buy. However, since lining paper does not have a pattern that must be matched, there is no need to allow extra rolls for this purpose.

Order of papering walls

● Always begin at the window.
● If there is more than one window, start at the window that gives most light.
● Work from the window to the longest unobstructed wall.
● Return to the other side of the window and hang lengths along the other wall.
● Centre pattern on a focal point like a chimney breast.
● Hang lengths round obstacles like doors, windows, pipes and fittings using the methods shown on pages 77–8.

Lining the walls

The method of hanging lining paper is similar to that of wallpaper except that it is best hung horizontally to give a smooth finish. This makes it difficult to handle on a long wall, so it should be folded, without creasing, like a concertina, pasted side to pasted side. Paste the rough side so smooth side is uppermost.

Measure the wall and cut lengths, adding 5cm for easing and trimming at each end. (If your walls are crooked, allow more to avoid gaps at the corners.)

1　Paste the lining paper and fold it concertina-style, without creasing, pasted side to pasted side. Leave the length for a few minutes to absorb moisture and to become supple.

2　Carry paper over an arm to wall and open top fold. Starting in right-hand corner, hold paper in left hand, brush to wall with the right (reverse if left-handed). Butt the joins.

Cutting the lengths

Cut full lengths needed to cover the room. Cut lengths round doors and window as you come to them.

Unroll paper right side upwards. Measure length required and add 5cm for trimming and easing at top and bottom.

Cut plain paper as for lining paper (see above).
Cut patterned paper as below to match pattern economically.

1　Find first complete pattern and cut first length so that, after final trimming, the main motif is at the top of the wall.

2　From first roll, cut first length and mark '1' on back. Cut exactly matching lengths and mark in odd numbers.

3　Unroll second roll by first, matching pattern. Cut exactly matching lengths and mark in even numbers.

Pasting

After all the lengths are cut, stack them in numerical order. Before each length is pasted, roll it the opposite way to the curl—it is much easier to paste lengths that are completely flat.
Ready-pasted and paste-the-wall coverings See next page.
Other wall coverings Paste as shown below, using the correct type of adhesive; check the manufacturer's advice on the roll of wall covering or the packet of adhesive.

If at all possible, set up your pasting board parallel to the window and face the window when pasting, so that the strong daylight will show up clearly any unpasted areas. If the length is not completely covered with adhesive, you may discover air bubbles or parting seams when decorating is complete.

Mix the adhesive as described on page 71. Apply the adhesive liberally, then brush out towards the edges of the wall covering. Check for unpasted areas and repaste if necessary. Wipe off any adhesive immediately from the right side of the length—keep a clean, dry cloth handy—or the wall covering could well be permanently marked.

Set pasted lengths aside to 'rest' that is, to allow the covering to become supple. For the resting time, follow the manufacturer's instructions.

1   Line up the covering with the furthest edge of the table, letting it overhang a little so that the table top is kept free of paste. Apply adhesive liberally down the centre.

2   Brush the paste out to the far edge of the paper, then slide the paper so the unpasted half overhangs the near side of the table. Brush paste from the centre to the near edge.

3   Fold over the pasted paper to half way, without creasing it. Slide the length of paper until the unpasted part is flush with the table top, the furthest edge overhanging as before.

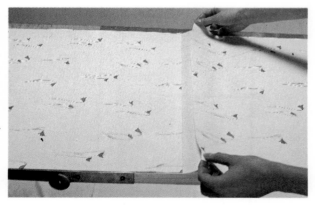

4   Paste the unpasted paper and fold to the first fold. Allow the paper to rest for the recommended time. Carry the folded paper to the wall with the first fold uppermost.

Ready-pasted wall coverings

No pasting table, bucket and brush are needed for ready-pasted papers so there is a great saving of time and potential mess. Cut the lengths as on page 73 and roll them up loosely from the bottom, with the pattern on the inside. The roll is then placed briefly in a cardboard trough of water—provided with the roll—to activate the paste.

Unless the walls are very uneven, there is no need to line when using ready-pasted vinyl since the backing acts as a lining. However, size the bare plaster.

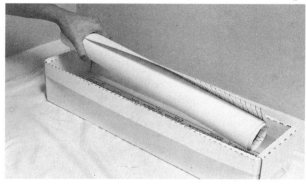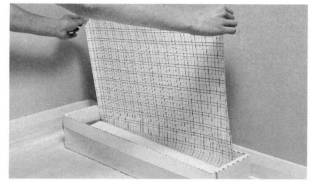

1 Place the water trough at base of wall and fill with water. Immerse rolled length of paper as instructed on the roll and agitate the water a little so that entire surface is soaked.

2 Slowly draw paper out of the trough, allowing surplus water to drain off. Position it and ease into place with a sponge, working out from the centre.

Paste-the-wall covering

This light-weight polythene film is very easy to hang. Do not cut and paste individual lengths. Instead, paste the wall with the special fungicidal adhesive which is recommended by the manufacturer—look on the roll. Then simply hang the covering, cut to length—allow 5cm as on page 76 and match the pattern. Never overlap the covering since it will not adhere. Avoid getting adhesive on to the covering since marks are very difficult to remove.

1 Size the walls with adhesive and allow to dry. Paste one wall at a time, using a pasting brush. Paste the corners and edges of wall with a paint pad or small brush.

2 While the paste is still wet, apply the wall covering from dry roll, without cutting into lengths. Start at top, unroll and smooth out with damp sponge. Trim as for other wall coverings.

Putting up

Hang the lengths as shown on this page. In general, lengths should not be overlapped, but butted carefully against each other. If you have to overlap, do so towards the light and smooth the seam with a roller.

Never hang lengths round corners—the corner will only be a weak point (see pages 77-8). Instead, cut the length so that about 10mm curves round the corner. Then hang the rest of the length on the adjacent wall, butting against the corner.

1 Chalk string and hang plumb line away from the wall. Pluck it against the wall to make a vertical line.

2 Hold top corners of paper and open up top half. Allowing 5cm for trimming, slide paper against plumb line.

3 Smooth along top of paper with brush, then smooth down the middle, working out to the edges. Open bottom fold and smooth down, leaving a trimming margin at the bottom.

4 Score the covering at the join of the ceiling and wall with the back of the scissors. Ease from wall and cut along score line, brush back down. Repeat at skirting edge.

5 Slide the next length alongside the first, butting up against it so patterns match and joins are hardly visible. Wipe off excess paste. Smooth length into place with the brush.

6 If edges do not lie flat and butted, use a seam roller about 20 minutes after hanging. Roll it all the way down the joins. Apply gently to embossed or textured coverings.

Problem areas

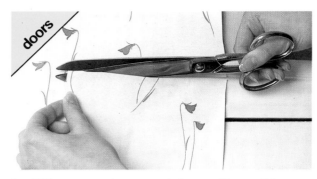

1 When papering round doors, if possible paste and hang a whole width of covering round the door for a good fit. Cut round the door to within about 5cm all round.

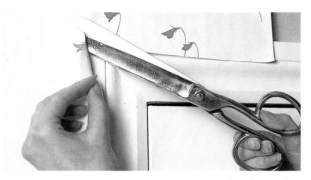

2 At the top corners of the door, clip into the paper diagonally. Cut about 6cm beyond the door frame. This will enable the paper to fit snugly round the frame.

3 Smooth the covering flat with the brush and press it well down round the outside of the door frame with the edges of the brush bristles to fit the covering exactly.

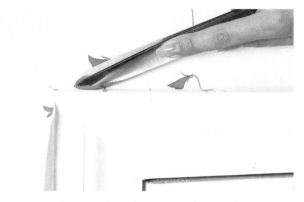

4 Score the overlapping covering at the top and bottom and round the door frame with the back of the scissors. Pull back the edges of the covering and trim rough edges. Press down.

1 Smooth covering down lightly over fitting. Pierce covering at the centre and make four cuts in the shape of a star, ending 2.5cm beyond the fitting edge.

2 Brush the covering down close to the fitting all round. Mark the edge of the fitting with the back of the scissors. Draw the flaps aside cut along the scored edges.

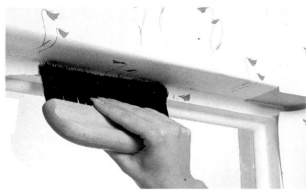

1 Measure into the window recess, allowing 6mm for trimming. Hang covering to plumb line and make a horizontal cut 6mm below recess. Brush covering into recess. Trim.

2 Cut and hang a short length of covering for the wall over the window, allowing 6mm for trimming window edge. Hang it alongside the one already in place. Brush into recess and trim.

3 Cut a patch to fit the gap left at the top of the window recess, matching the pattern. Make sure the patch fits over the whole gap, including the 6mm space at the top of recess.

4 Smooth down the 6mm flap over the new patch to fit snugly in the recess. Smooth the covering over the angle of the recess with your finger tips—make sure your hands are clean.

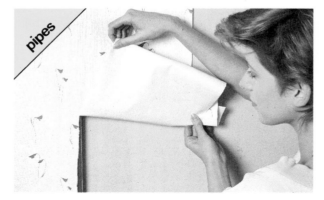

1 Paste the length and hang it over the pipe. Smooth down lightly and cut the covering up the middle over the pipe, thus dividing the covering in two.

2 Ease the two sections so they fit neatly behind the pipe. Press down with a brush, tucking the covering well behind the pipe so that the join is hidden and the covering is smooth.

Papering a ceiling

Papered ceilings can be used to create many interesting effects, but working overhead to line and paper a ceiling can be an arduous job, unless working conditions are comfortable and safe. This means building a walkway that allows you to work near to the ceiling without over-stretching yourself, while considering the safety aspects of working at heights. Ideally you should have two step-ladders which can hold a plank which is long and strong enough to support two people, giving you free movement.

Start with a smallish room, so that you will not be handling a large amount of wallpaper overhead. Once you have developed a reasonable technique for working on ceilings, you may wish to move on to more adventurous (and difficult) projects. Avoid the heavier wall coverings which can be cumbersome to handle without experience.

Choosing materials

Lining paper should first be used where the ceiling has particularly hard plaster, where the surface has been oil-painted, creating a completely impervious surface, if the ceiling has undergone an excessive amount of 'making good' with particularly uneven surfaces, or where a very expensive wall covering is to be used.

The range of lining papers is limited—plain ones are suitable for a blemish-free ceiling, while the woodchip types are better for camouflaging a less-than-perfect surface. Lining paper is normally hung across the line of the ceiling paper and must be butted very carefully so that the joins will not show through the decorative paper itself. Make sure the lining has dried out completely before hanging the new wall covering.

If you are going to hang vinyl paper on top, you should always use a fungicidal adhesive to hang both the vinyl and the lining paper. This will eliminate the chance of moisture becoming trapped between the ceiling and papers and possibly producing mould patches in the future; these would obviously ruin your decorating.

Embossed papers such as Anaglypta and Superglypta create interesting decorative effects which are highlighted with a paint finish. They are also used to disguise less-than-perfect surfaces. However, they can be extremely heavy to hold at heights once the adhesive has been applied. These really need to be applied by two people, so that one can support the paper while the other slides it into position.

Another problem with using heavily embossed papers is that unless you have applied enough adhesive to allow easy movement across the ceiling, you can damage the raised pattern by pressing it down too firmly when handling it during the process of hanging.

Paste-the-wall coverings can be fixed easily on to ceilings. The ceiling is pasted first and the paper pressed down on to the pasted surface, making such papers ideal for ceilings. Once the paper has been cut to length, reroll the cut length so that the pattern is inside. The paper will be lightweight to handle, and is a particularly good choice for the beginner.

Vinyls are particularly suitable for any steamy or condensation-prone areas, like kitchens and bathrooms. They are washable, but need a fungicidal adhesive to prevent moisture problems later on. Also, because they are very pliable, they will help disguise a slightly uneven ceiling.

Ready-pasteds are more complicated to use on ceilings, since the paper is unrolled from a water trough and pressed directly on to the surface. The sheer mechanics of the job make it difficult to paper a ceiling successfully using these types of paper. In any event, do not use cheap ready-pasted paper, which tends to stretch if over-handled and may also bleed its dye, causing a blotchy effect.

The first time you paper a ceiling, choose a small room and a lightweight, but reasonable quality paper so that you don't have to handle a large amount of heavy paper.

CHAPTER 3

Upholstery

This chapter deals with four fairly simple upholstery projects that yield both professional and stylish results. With the advent of modern materials such as foam and rubber the craft of upholstery has been made easier for the beginner. By following the step-by-step instructions you will be able to renovate all kinds of upholstered furniture, both traditional—stuffed and sprung—or modern. The best introduction for the complete novice is to re-make the drop-in seat of a dining chair, moving on to more complicated projects such as renewing a sprung seat using traditional materials, re-upholstering a modern armchair and making a beautiful deep-buttoned headboard for your bed—the height of luxury and comfort.

Replacing a drop-in seat

If buying your chair, make sure the frame is basically sound. Before starting, clean it with white spirit on a rag. Broken joints can be repaired and loose joints tapped back into place, but look out for woodworm. Holes and little piles of sawdust will betray they are alive. Treat the wood with woodworm fluid, following the instructions on the tin. Fill the treated holes with wood filler or with plastic wood, first coloured to match.

Buying the materials

Webbing goes across the seat frame and supports the foam pad. Two strands each way are needed

A new look for dining chairs. Before newly upholstered seats were replaced, the chairs were treated with wood bleach and varnish.

One of the chairs before recovering. They were dirty and were cleaned with a cloth dampened with white spirit. The joints were reglued then tapped in place and they were treated with woodworm killer.

for a small chair, three for a larger chair. Buy good quality webbing. Pure flax is best, with a twill-weave, recognizable by its diagonal lines.

Foam padding is inexpensive and comes in many thicknesses. For a drop-in seat, use dense, 5cm-thick foam.

Buy good quality hessian, thick and closely woven, as used by upholsterers. This lines the underside of the frame.

Cotton or linen lining fabric protects the foam. Use old but not badly worn, cotton or linen sheets, or calico, though this is thicker and will take up more space in the frame.

Upholstery-weight fabric is the best choice for the top cover, and should be colourfast with a firm, close weave. It should be easily cleaned. A supple, non-fray fabric is a good choice. Thick fabric such as leather will take up extra space.

How to tackle the upholstery

WHAT YOU NEED

Cover fabric	15mm webbing tacks	Towelling
Linen or cotton lining fabric	12mm tacks	Felt-tip pen and chalk
	Plastic wood	Wood (16cm × 5cm × 2cm)
Hessian	Fabric adhesive	
4 strips of linen or cotton	Hammer	Tape measure
Webbing	Old screwdriver	2 G-clamps
5cm-thick foam padding	Pincers	Plus: Cutting-out scissors

How to work out your quantities

Fabric: Measure the length and width of each seat at the widest points and allow at least 20cm longer and wider.
Linen or cotton lining: Measure as for cover fabric.
Foam padding: 1.2cm larger all round than seat frame. The foam should be 5cm deep.

Linen or cotton strips: Each strip is 10cm wide by length of one side of foam plus 15cm.
Hessian: Two pieces, the same size as the seat frame.
Webbing: Measure frame vertically and horizontally, double for a small seat, treble for a large, add 2.5cm per strip and 36cm to wind round the wood block.

1 Secure seat upside down on a work surface with G-clamps. Using screwdriver and hammer, drive out old tacks. Strip the seat. Clean frame and fill holes with filler.

2 Leave a space the width of webbing between each strip. Leaving 2.5cm surplus webbing, tack it to the back of the frame with three 15mm tacks.

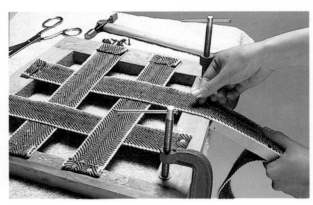

3 Wrap the free end of the webbing round wood block and stretch from back to front. Tack with a central 15mm tack, then with a 15mm tack on each side. Turn back fold as in Step 2.

4 The side webbing runs across the seat from side to side. Secure in the same way, but interlace the side strips with the first pieces of webbing to give the seat extra strength.

5 To cover the webbing and the underside of the seat, cut two pieces of hessian the same size as the frame. Place the frame on straight grain of the hessian and draw round it.

6 Cut out the lining and the cover using hessian shapes as a pattern, and allowing 10cm extra all round. Make sure grain is straight and pattern falls correctly on cover.

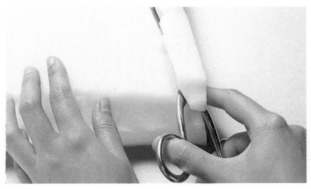

7 Tack one folded side of hessian to frame back with 12mm tacks every 4cm. Stretch to front then sides, fixing temporarily with 15mm tacks, then permanently with 12mm tacks.

8 Using cutting-out scissors, 'feather' the foam by cutting 25mm strips off the bottom perimeter of the pad. This will make it easier to achieve a rounded shape to the seat.

9 Fold each 10cm-wide strip of cotton in half lengthways and stick one half to the uncut perimeter of the foam. Stick strips down thoroughly or the fabric will form a ridge.

10 When dry, place the foam on the hessian-covered webbing, stuck sides uppermost and holding it firmly, turn frame upside down. Pull strips down tightly; temporarily tack.

11 Adjust and tighten tacks and when the foam is firmly squashed down all round, remove temporary tacks one at a time and tack with 12mm tacks. Trim strips at corners.

12 Pull down one corner and tack centrally with a 15mm tack. Pull the rest of the corner fabric into little pleats round the corner, tacking as you go. Trim excess with scissors.

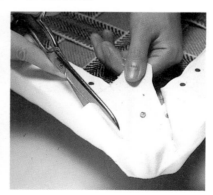

13 Cover the foam with lining, tacking with temporary then permanent tacks. Pull down corners. Tack.

14 Fold two side pleats towards the nail to form a neat corner. Crease the fabric firmly with your fingers.

15 Cut out the triangular section formed by pleats inside the crease line and along sides of nail.

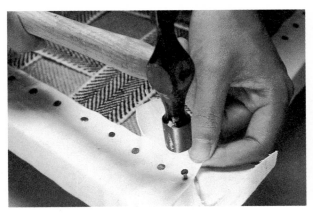

16 Fold in one of the side flaps and tack it down securely with 12mm tacks. Fold the second flap over the first and tack in the same way. Trim any untidy edges.

17 Fold cover fabric in half and mark the fold. Mark frame centre front and back. With seat foam-side down on wrong side of cover, line up marks and tack on cover as for lining.

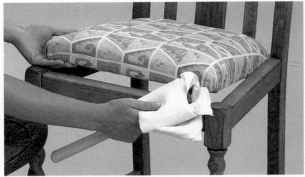

18 Tack hessian covering tightly to the underside of the frame, first with temporary 15mm tacks, then with 12mm tacks, folding in all the raw edges and corners.

19 Replace the finished seat in the chair frame, back edge first. It may be difficult to fit, so tap it lightly in place with a hammer well wrapped in cloth, when it should fit snugly.

Renewing a sprung seat

A sprung seat is a very common form of up-holstery and is found in a wide variety of chairs used for different purposes, such as in a bedroom, or dining room. It is not difficult to renew. All it requires is the right materials and tools, and a little patience to follow through each stage of the process. The method shown here uses traditional materials, although foam can be used instead of stuffing if you prefer. Follow Steps 1–22 pages 88–93 to renew a seat, and Steps 1–4 pages 93–4 to renew a back pad.

This Edwardian chair was basically sound, but in obvious need of attention. A new seat and cover transform it completely

Guide to materials and tools

Although upholstery requires a number of tools, these are readily available from craft and DIY shops and can be used for other jobs.

Upholstery fabric should be colourfast and hardwearing.

Braid covers the tacks and raw edges. A scroll braid or gimp, which looks like an elaborate ricrac braid, can be eased neatly round corners. Straight-edged braids must be folded in a mitre.

Calico is used to cover the wadding. It can also be used underneath the chair.

Wadding is placed over the scrim and stuffing to give the seat a smooth surface. Use a good cotton wadding.

Scrim is a lightweight hessian, used to cover the stuffing.

Stuffing is used to pad out the seat over the springs. Horsehair is the traditional stuffing, although vegetable fibres such as Algerian fibre (palm grass) and coconut fibre can also be used. Foam is another alternative.

Hessian is used to cover the springs. It can also be used instead of calico to cover the underneath of the chair.

Webbing must be strong to support the springs and stuffing. Buy a good quality webbing such as pure flax.

Tacks are available in two varieties: improved tacks, which have large heads, and fine tacks, with smaller heads. Use 15mm improved tacks for the webbing, 12mm fine tacks for several layers of fabric and 10mm fine tacks for single layers.

A ripping chisel is used for removing old tacks. An old chisel or screwdriver can also be used.

A wooden mallet should be used with a chisel.

An upholsterer's hammer is generally heavier than a normal woodworking hammer and is useful for hammering in large webbing tacks.

A webbing stretcher is used to pull the webbing taut while the tacks are hammered in. With the slot and peg stretcher, the webbing is pushed down through the slot to form a loop beneath it, and the peg is inserted through the peg loop, holding the webbing firm.

A curved needle is needed to stitch the springs to the webbing and hessian, and to work bridle tacks.

A mattress needle is a double-pointed needle used for tacking the stuffing in place, blind stitching and working the edge roll.

Twine is a strong, smooth thread, which does not stretch or break. It is used to tie the springs to the webbing and hessian, blind stitching and edge-stitching.

Fabric adhesive is used to secure the braid to the cover. Choose a clear adhesive which takes a few minutes to set, so you can reposition the braid if necessary.

A craft knife is essential for cutting twine and trimming the fabric to size. Choose one with replaceable blades so it is always sharp.

How to tackle the upholstery

1 Using a chisel and mallet, remove the tacks holding the old cover and seating in place. Cut through the twine with a sharp craft knife. Remove any tacks left in the frame.

2 Upturn the chair on an old table to remove the old webbing. Replace, working from a continuous length, using a webbing stretcher or tensioning block.

WHAT YOU NEED

Cover fabric
Braid
Calico
Wadding
Scrim
Horsehair or vegetable fibre
Hessian
Webbing
15mm improved tacks
12mm and 10mm fine tacks
Ripping chisel, old chisel or screwdriver

Wooden mallet
Upholstery hammer or ordinary
  hammer
Webbing stretcher or piece of wood 16cm
  × 5cm × 2cm
Large curved needle
Mattress needle
Twine
Fabric adhesive
Sharp craft knife
Plus: Cutting-out scissors, small sewing
scissors, tape measure, dressmaker's pins

How to work out your quantities

Fabric If the old cover is in a reasonable condition, it can often be removed and used as a pattern. If this is not possible, take the dimensions of the seat at the widest points, with the old covering still in place. Measure from the fabric edge at one side of the frame to the fabric edge at the other, and then from front to back in the same way. Allow an extra 5cm or more all round, so the cover can be trimmed to size on the chair. (This also applies when using the old cover as a pattern.) If you are using a patterned fabric, remember to allow for centring the design on the seat. It may help to make a pattern of the seat in tracing paper so you can find the best position on the fabric, before buying.
Braid Measure around the edge of the seat frame and allow 10cm extra for neatening.
Calico Measure the top of the seat as for

the cover fabric, and then the frame on the underside of the chair in the same way, adding 5cm all round for neatening. Allow extra if you are using foam instead of stuffing.
Wadding Measure as for the cover fabric, and allow twice this quantity for two layers.
Scrim and hessian Measure as for cover fabric. Omit the scrim if using foam.
Stuffing This is bought by weight. A 1kg bag is more than enough for one seat.
Webbing Measure across the frame at each of the original webbing positions. Add 2.5cm to each length for turnings, and an extra 15cm to the total to enable you to use a webbing stretcher. (Allow 36cm extra if using an improvized wooden tensioning block.)

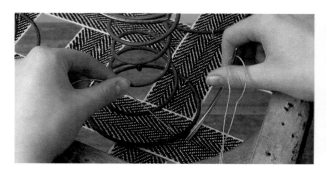

3 Turn the chair upright and reposition the springs. Stitch to the webbing using a curved needle and a long length of twine, securing the first stitch with a slip knot.

4 Hammer 15mm webbing tacks halfway into the frame, in line with each spring. Make a slip knot in a long length of twine, leaving a 20cm end. Place over a tack at back of frame.

5 Pull the knot tight and hammer in the tack. Compress the spring by 5cm and tie the long end round second coil. Take through the spring and tie to the top coil at the far side.

6 Compress second spring. Knot twine on top coil and then on second coil. Tie off on the appropriate front tack, leaving a 20cm length hanging free. Hammer in the tack.

7 Repeat with the remaining pair of springs, and then across the width of the seat. Knot the 20cm ends of twine round the top coil of each spring and tie to give a rounded profile.

8 Cut the hessian roughly to size and place over springs. Fold edges back and tack to upper edge of chair frame with 12mm tacks, tensioning slightly. Trim edges to about 4cm.

9 Using a curved needle and twine, stitch the springs to the hessian in the same way as they were stitched to the webbing. Secure the first and last stitches with a slip knot.

10 Secure the end of the twine to one corner. Using a curved needle, make large stitches around the edge of the seat, loose enough to take three fingers on edge.

11 Tease out the horsehair or fibre and force handfuls under the bridle ties. Fill in the centre until the seat is completely covered with a layer approximately 15cm deep.

12 Cover the stuffing with a piece of scrim. Tuck raw edges under the stuffing and tack to the bevelled edge of the chair frame, following the grain to ensure a straight edge.

13 Thread a mattress needle with twine and stitch through the scrim and stuffing using large tacking stitches. Stitch around the seat, 7.5cm from the edge, ending in the centre.

14 To give the seat a firm edge, work one or two rows of blind stitching using a mattress needle and twine. Work in an anti-clockwise direction, starting at the back.

To start the blind stitching, insert the needle just above the tacks, 2.5cm from the back strut. Push it through at 45° so the point appears about 5cm from the edge. Stop before the eye is visible and push it back, making it reappear slightly to the left of the first stitch. Make a slip knot and pull tight.

Insert the needle 5cm to the right of the knot, as before. Push it back so it emerges half way between the stitch and the slip knot. Before pulling it out completely, make two or three turns of twine round the needle and pull tight. Continue round the seat in the same way.

If the height of the seat is more than 7.5cm make a second row of stitching 2cm above the first.

An edge roll is worked in a similar way to blind stitching and pulls the stuffing to the sides of the seat to give a firm edge. Starting on the left side, and pinching the edge together, insert a mattress needle into the lower guideline at a 45° angle so it emerges through the upper guideline. Pull through completely and reinsert on the upper line, slightly to the left of the first stitch. Secure with a slip knot.

Insert the needle 2.5cm to the right of the knot and pull out on the upper line. Reinsert needle on the upper line, half way between the knot and the stitch. Pull through, wrapping the twine round the needle. Continue round the edge of the seat in the same way.

15 To make an edge roll, mark guidelines about 2.5cm apart around the top and sides of the seat. Pinch together and stitch from the back of the chair.

16 Cut a piece of wadding slightly larger than the top of the seat and place on top of the hessian to fill in the depressions made by the stitches holding the stuffing in place.

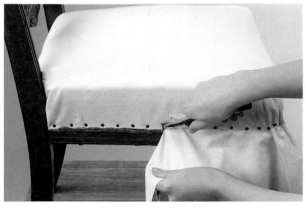

17 Cut calico at least 5cm larger than the seat all round, and tack over the wadding, fitting round the back struts (see Step 19), and pleating the corners. Trim with a knife.

18 Cover calico with a second layer of wadding. Iron the new covering, cut at least 5cm larger than the seat all round, and position on the seat, centring the pattern.

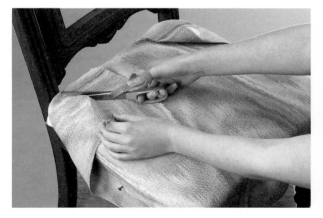

19 Hold the cover in place by hammering 15mm webbing tacks halfway into the frame. Turn back corners at back of seat and cut to within 1cm of fold. Fit around struts.

20 Trim excess fabric from back corners, leaving enough to turn under. Tack the cover in place, close to the decorative edge, making a neat fold at the front corners.

21 Apply fabric adhesive to the tacked edge of the cover and the wrong side of the braid. Position the braid around the edge of the seat, turning under raw edges at each end.

22 Upturn the chair and tack a piece of calico to the frame to make a dust cover. Turn under the raw edges and fit round the legs in the same way as the cover fabric (Step 19).

How to upholster a back pad

WHAT YOU NEED
Cover fabric
Braid
Calico
Wadding
12mm and 10mm fine tacks
Ripping chisel, old woodworking
   chisel or screwdriver

Wooden mallet
Upholstery hammer or ordinary
   hammer
Fabric adhesive
Sharp knife
Plus: Cutting-out scissors, small sewing
scissors, tape measure, dressmaker's pins

How to work out your quantities
Fabric
Measure the width and depth of the pad. Cut one piece slightly smaller than these dimensions (5mm less all round), and one piece slightly larger (2cm more all round). If using a patterned fabric, remember to allow for centring the pattern on the back

pad when calculating the fabric amounts.
Calico Measure the width and depth of the back pad and cut one piece of calico 5mm less all round.
Wadding Cut two pieces same size as calico.
Braid Measure around the edge of the back pad and allow 5cm extra for neatening.

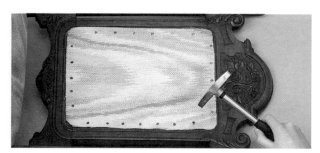

1 Cut two pieces of fabric for the back pad, one slightly smaller and one slightly larger than the area. Tack the smaller piece to the frame, with the wrong side uppermost.

2 Cut two pieces of wadding and one piece of calico slightly smaller than the area. Place both layers of wadding and then the calico under the fabric and tack in place.

3 Cover the calico with the remaining piece of fabric, cut slightly larger than the area, and tack as close as possible to the edge, leaving enough room to trim the edges with a knife.

4 Attach the braid round the edge of the back pad using fabric adhesive. Ease or mitre the corners and finish by turning under the braid and overlapping it over the raw edge.

The back of the chair shows the reverse side of the back pad, with the pattern centred. Check the fabric you choose is suitable for upholstery so that you can be sure it will wear well. Co-ordinate it with the colours and patterns in the room.

Renewing a modern armchair

Modern shaped armchairs can be quickly rejuvenated using contemporary materials and techniques where each section of the chair is built up and completed in turn.

The first task is to strip off all the original upholstery to the frame and remove the castors (if any), since it is much easier to work on a stable chair. Any loose joints should be glued and all old tacks removed. If the chair has a stuffing rail (under the bottom arm rail), this can also be removed as it is unnecessary for modern upholstery. Use a rasp or sandpaper to smooth the corners of the frame, especially on the arm rests and on the back and seat rails, to protect the new materials from unnecessary wear. Check that the back seat rail is the correct height for foam padding. If springs were used before, this rail may need raising to allow roughly one finger width between the top edge of the back seat rail and the bottom edge of the bottom back rail. You can use the existing fixings to do this.

Finally, before beginning, study the diagram 'Parts of the chair frame' and familiarize yourself with the names.

The chair with its original, very worn, vinyl covering. Chairs of a similar shape and type can be bought from second-hand shops or auctions quite cheaply, or you could be lucky enough to find one forgotten in the loft.

The same chair once it has been stripped of the old upholstery, the frame has been sanded and the first stage of the new upholstery has been completed.

Materials guide

Cover fabric: Upholstery fabrics with smooth, glazed or pile surfaces can be used, as well as leather (cowhide) or imitation leather (a woven cloth base with a sprayed-on plastic coating). For a first attempt it is better to use conventional upholstery fabric before tackling the tougher types of covering. Choose a firmly woven fabric and when you know the width, make a cutting plan to ensure you buy the most economical amount. Plain-coloured fabrics or small all-over repeat patterns are easier to handle and cheaper to use than very large repeats since the latter must be centred on each section of the chair and so you will need extra fabric.

Hardboard or plywood: Both are light and strong and make ideal materials for filling the areas of the frame where firm support is needed—for example, inside the arms—and which will later be padded with foam. Local DIY suppliers will usually cut pieces free of charge to customer's particular specifications For shapes other than squares or rectangles, it is best to make a full-size paper pattern or card template first; otherwise, take a plan showing exact measurements.

Cardboard: Light, firm mounting board is used to cover the outside arms and the bottom front edge of the chair and keeps the finished weight to a minimum. It is sold in sheets of different sizes and thicknesses and can easily be cut to shape with scissors, or a knife and steel edge, and then tacked or stapled in place.

Foam padding: This is available in two main qualities. The plain variety is sold in different

How to tackle the upholstery

WHAT YOU NEED

1 Cover fabric
2 3mm-thick hardboard or plywood
3 2mm to 3mm-thick cardboard
4 1.5cm-thick foam (light seat density) for arm fronts, back side pieces and seat cover
5 2.5cm-thick foam (light seat density) for inside arm cover
6 5cm-thick foam (medium back density) for back pad of chair
7 2.5cm-thick chipfoam (medium density) for armrests
8 3.5cm-thick chipfoam (medium density) for lower back rest
9 5cm-thick chipfoam (firm density) for seat
10 2oz synthetic wadding
11 Cotton stockinette
12 Calico
13 Hessian
14 5cm-wide rubber webbing
15 2cm-long wire nails
16 10mm and 13mm improved tacks
17 Back tack strip
18 Upholsterer's 75mm circular needle, 17 or 19 gauge (fine)
19 Upholsterer's skewers

Plus: Soft pencil and ruler, rasp or medium-coarse sandpaper, general-purpose wood saw, towel or blanket for work table, ripping chisel or old screwdriver and mallet, foam adhesive, block of wood about 8cm × 8cm × 20cm, foam cushion pad (10cm deep at dome reducing to 9cm at edges), fabric shears, glass-topped pins, tape measure, matching zip for cushion cover, No 18 linen thread to match top fabric, upholsterer's hammer.

How to work out your quantities

Cover fabric: Block—that is, squared-off—measurements are first taken of each section of the chair and the fabric cut out. The cover pieces are then precisely shaped over the foam at the fitting stage. For all outside pieces, measure across the widest point and add 8cm all round. For the inside-back cover, measure the width of the back and add 5cm to each side. For side back and front arm facings, allow 3cm extra all round.

widths and thicknesses and is graded as seat or back density (seat density is the firmest). The second type, chipfoam, is a dense composite quality sold in different widths and two grades of density, medium and firm. It is used to give firm support under a top cover of plain foam.

Foam cushion pads: These are very firm. The best are domed. They are available in two standard sizes, 51cm square, or 50cm wide at the front, tapering to 47cm at the back by 56cm long by 9cm deep. To get an exact fit, the pads can either be cut down, or built up by gluing on small strips of foam evenly at opposite sides to ensure that the dome remains in the exact centre.

Cotton stockinette: A knitted tubular fabric available in different widths and in a neutral colour. It is used to cover the foam cushion pad and prevents the top fabric from slipping, wrinkling or clinging and leaving hollows when the cushion is depressed.

Synthetic wadding: Available in different widths, usually 70cm and 140cm wide, and in several weights. It is used to cover the foam to give a smooth overall surface to the shape of the chair before fitting on the top fabric.

Calico: This is used to shape the back foam over the curved top of the back of the chair.

Hessian: This is used to cover the underneath of the chair and acts as a dust cover.

Rubber webbing: Sold by the metre in 4cm and 5cm widths, in black, grey or fawn.

Upholsterer's skewers: Long steel pins available in 8cm and 10.5cm lengths. They are used for pinning through the upholstery when fitting the fabric in place.

Zip fastener: Choose the correct weight and colour to match the top fabric.

Linen thread: This is available from upholstery suppliers. It is a strong thread, used to sew the different sections of the top cover together.

For inside edges where the seat meets the arms, allow 15cm for wrapping around the rails. Measure for the cushion covers in the normal way.

Hardboard or plywood: Measure the width and height of the inside arm just inside the top and bottom rails and between the chair front and back rail. Double this amount for the total amount needed for both sides.

Cardboard: On the outside of the chair, measure the length of the top arm rail and the distance between the top arm rail and the under arm rail. Add 2cm to the distance between rails to allow for a strip for backtacking. Double this amount for both sides. Similarly, measure the width and height of the chair front between the front seat rail and the front bottom rail. Add the two quantities together to give the total amount needed.

Foam padding: Measure at the widest points of the chair to give the basic quantities of foam needed. The foam can then be trimmed to the exact shape on the chair or cut to shape beforehand with the help of a paper template. Use a sharp craft knife or an electric carving knife to cut the foam. For arm fronts, measure the width of the front of the arm across the widest point and add 2.5cm to the length. Double this amount for both sides. For the side back pieces, measure the length and width of the two side back rails. For the top seat cover, measure from underside of back seat rail to bottom of front bottom rail, and around seat rails at each side. For inside arms, measure from bottom of bottom arm rail up over arm to under arm rail and from front to back. For the back, measure the height of the back from the top rail to the bottom rail and add 2.5cm. Measure the width to the outside edges of the back uprights and add 2cm to each side. For the lower back rest, measure along the back upright from top arm rail to the bottom of the bottom back rail, and subtract 5cm. Measure the distance between the two back uprights at the level of the under arm rail. For each arm rest, measure both ways and add 1cm to side edges. For the seat, measure from the inside of the back seat rail to the front of the front seat rail, then across the seat width.

Cotton stockinette: Measure the cushion pad across the widest point and add an extra 4cm.

Synthetic wadding: For each arm, measure from outside the bottom arm rail round the arm to the under arm rail, and the width inside plus the width across the front of the arm. For the seat, measure from outside the back rail to the bottom of the front bottom rail, and the width around the two side rails. For the back, measure from inside of bottom rail to outside of top back rail and from the back of the back uprights at the widest point.

Rubber webbing: For the average armchair, allow four or five webs down the back and five or six down the seat (measured half way inside the rails), two webs across the back above the arms, and about three across the seat. Make webs about 15cm longer at each side of seat for tacking around the side rails.

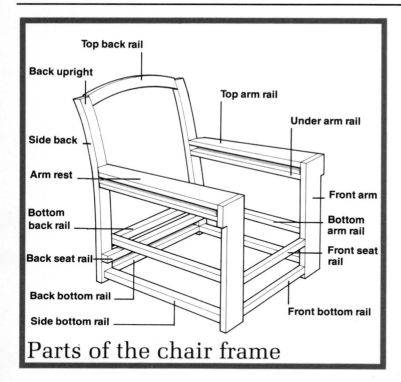

Parts of the chair frame

Top back rail
Back upright
Side back
Arm rest
Bottom back rail
Back seat rail
Back bottom rail
Side bottom rail
Top arm rail
Under arm rail
Front arm
Bottom arm rail
Front seat rail
Front bottom rail

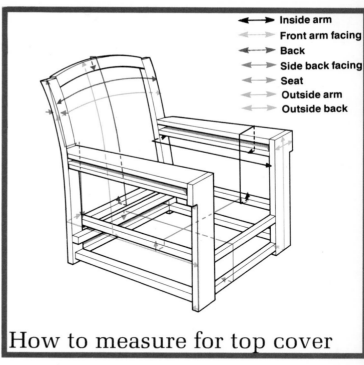

How to measure for top cover

Inside arm
Front arm facing
Back
Side back facing
Seat
Outside arm
Outside back

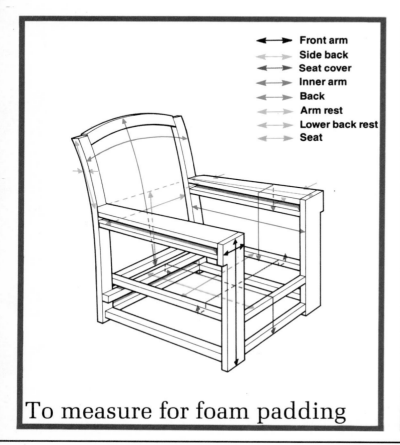

To measure for foam padding

Front arm
Side back
Seat cover
Inner arm
Back
Arm rest
Lower back rest
Seat

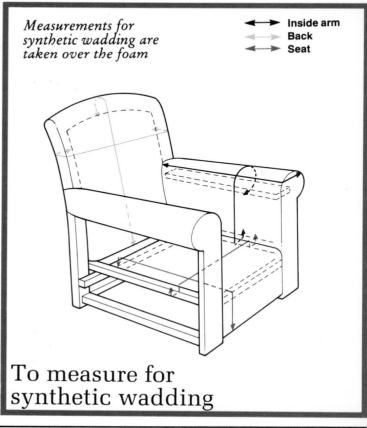

Measurements for synthetic wadding are taken over the foam

Inside arm
Back
Seat

To measure for synthetic wadding

Cutting plan for 137cm-wide top fabric

Inside arm	Inside arm	Outside arm	Outside arm	Cushion top	Cushion bottom				
					Side back facing				
					Side back facing				
Outside back	Inside back	Seat		Front arm facing	Side gusset	Side gusset	Back gussets	Front gusset	
				Front arm facing					

1 Strip the chair and remove all the old tacks. Fit hardboard to inside of arms with rough side uppermost. Fix, using 2cm wire nails and sand the edges smooth.

2 Fill in the space between the top arm rail and the under arm rail with card cut to size. Fix in place with 10mm or 13mm tacks spaced 10cm apart all round the edge.

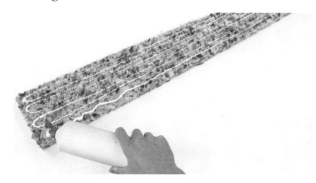

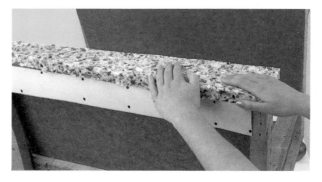

3 Cut 2.5cm chipfoam to fit arm rests and apply foam adhesive to one side, working in rows along the length. Take care to glue right up to the edges all round.

4 Apply foam to arm rests with a staple gun. Make sure the front edge is flush with front arm and the side edges overhang slightly to soften the edges of the arm rests. Trim if necessary.

5 Cut 1.5cm foam to fit front arms and glue one side as far as level of seat rail. Stick to front arms, aligning top edge with top edge of chipfoam on arm rests.

6 Glue chipfoam and hardboard. Apply inside arm foam with lower edge to bottom arm rail, and front edge to front arm. Tack to bottom arm rail through thickness of foam.

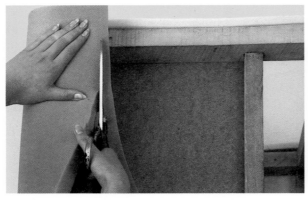

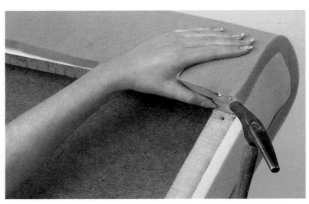

7 Smooth foam over the top of the arm, tensioning slightly. Trim outer edge of foam to shape, following the lower edge of the under arm rail, on outside of arm.

8 Apply adhesive to card and side edge of foam on front arm. Smooth foam over arm so front edges are flush, and tack to under arm rail through thickness of foam.

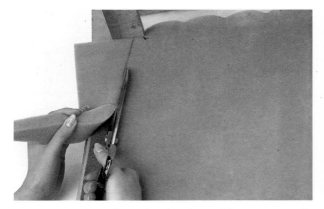

9 Draw a line from back edge of foam at inside of arm to centre of bottom back rail. Trim foam along the line to allow for back padding. Tack to hardboard.

10 Position inner arm fabric on arm, and pin to front arm facing, following the edge of the arm. Trim, remove from chair and stitch together with right sides facing.

11 Lay wadding over arm, from bottom arm rail on inside to under arm rail on outside. Bring round front arm and trim top to a curve. Hold in place with a few tacks.

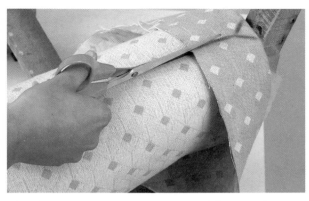

12 Fit inner arm cover over wadding and temporarily tack at front and back. Turn back fabric at back upright and make a cut so the fabric can be fitted round the frame.

13 Tension fabric diagonally to back and temporarily tack to back upright. Make cut to back seat rail, tension fabric under bottom arm rail and tack in place.

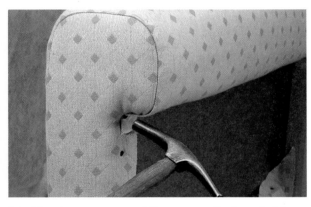

14 Cut into corner of front arm facing, fold fabric back and bring top fabric round over it. Tack to underside of under arm rail. Tack back edges to back of back upright.

To fit the inner arm cover, cut fabric to centre of back upright, finishing 2.5cm from fold, then make diagonal cuts out to the edges of the upright. Turn under flap and raw edges at each side. Tension round upright and temporarily tack to back. Make the same cut to the front seat rail. Fold under front facing along seamline and temporarily tack to front bottom rail. Tack flap to top of front seat rail.

The completed armchair is totally transformed by a contemporary fabric.

How to complete the upholstery

Note: Arrow denotes the direction of the top of the armchair.

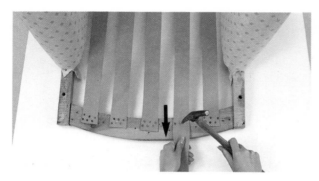

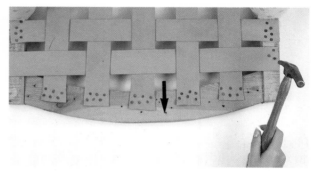

1 Attach five lengths of rubber webbing to back of chair, with canvas side uppermost. Tack to bottom back rail, then stretch and fix to top back rail, using six 13mm tacks.

2 Weave two lengths of webbing across the back, positioning the first just above the arms, and the second just below the top back rail. Tension and tack in place as before.

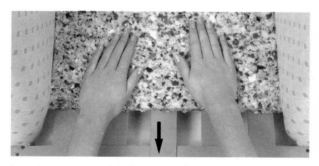

3 Cut 3.5cm chipfoam to fit lower part of back and bevel top and bottom edges. Stick to webbing so bottom aligns with top of bottom back rail.

4 Cut 1.5cm foam to fit side back rails, and stick in place. Cut 5cm foam to fit back and glue in place, aligning the side back edges with edge of foam on side back rails.

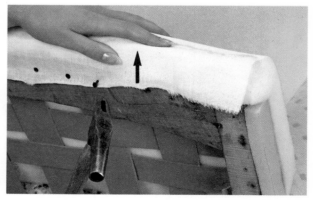

5 Tack bottom edge of foam to inside edge of bottom back rail, tacking through the thickness of the foam, and working from the centre to each side.

6 Glue a 10cm-wide calico strip to the top edge of the foam. Pull to the back of the top back rail, shaping the foam over the back edge. Tack calico in place using 10mm tacks.

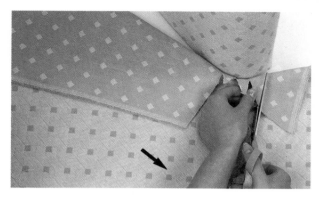

7 Centre inside back fabric on back and temporarily tack at centre of top and bottom back rails. Fold back fabric to meet top inner edge of arm and cut to ease round curve.

8 Mark cutting line 1.5cm from curve. Fit side pieces (see Step 10, page 100), remove and stitch to entire length of side edges of back with right sides facing.

9 Fit wadding and top cover on back of chair. With corner in position, make a cut 2.5cm in from corner towards centre of back upright, ending 5cm from seam (see Step 12, page 101).

10 Push side back facing under edge of foam at top of arm, then make a cut to top of bottom back rail, as before. Push round foam and pull facing through to back of chair.

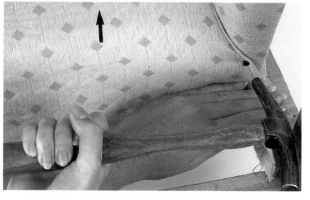

11 Fit side back pieces round back upright, tucking under raw edges where the cut was made, and pulling back and down to avoid pulls in the fabric. Temporarily tack in place.

12 Pull bottom edge of back top cover down and out to the sides of the chair, tensioning evenly. Temporarily tack to the underside of lower arm rail at each side.

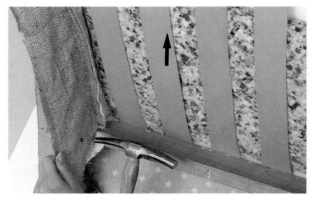

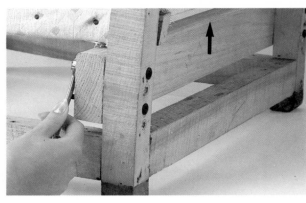

13 Bring fly attached to side back piece through to back of chair, pulling down and out. Temporarily tack to inside of back upright. Finish tacking and trim off excess fabric.

14 Fix back seat rail to back uprights to leave a finger space below the bottom back rail. Push bolts through from the back and tighten nuts on the inside of the chair.

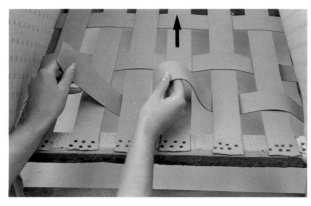

15 Run six lengths of webbing from back of back seat rail to top of front seat rail. Weave three lengths across and temporarily tack to outside edges of bottom arm rails.

16 Apply glue to webbing and position 5cm chipfoam on seat so it meets top fabric at arms and back and comes slightly over the front seat rail. Hold firm until thoroughly stuck.

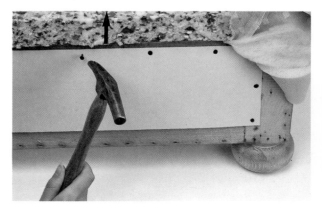

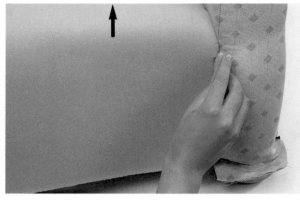

17 Fix card to the front of the chair, tacking to front seat rail and front bottom rail. Lift foam, wadding and top fabric on front arms to tack card in place at each side.

18 Glue 1.5cm foam to seat and fit round front seat rail. Release webbing and push through sides and back of chair. Mark cutting line at front, trim and glue to card.

19 Cover with wadding, then top fabric. Cut fabric to fit round front seat rail and push through sides of chair. Pleat corners and tack. Glue front arm foam over fabric.

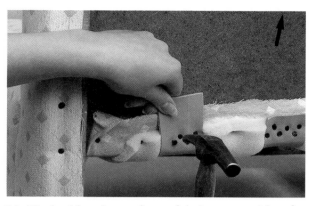

20 Tack side edges of seat fabric to outside of bottom arm rail. Fold up wadding and foam and tack at 10cm intervals. Trim. Tension webbing and tack to rail through all thicknesses.

21 Cover front arm foam with wadding and tuck fabric behind wadding, folding on stitching line. Using a curved needle and linen thread, hemstitch to front fabric edge.

22 Turn chair upside down and place outside arm fabric right side down on underarm. Position back tack strip from front to back of arm and tack in place through fabric.

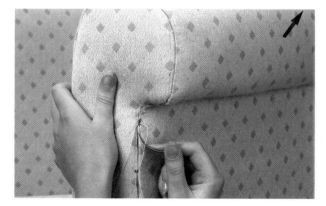

23 Cover bottom rail and back uprights with wadding. Tension cover to bottom rail and tack. Fold under front edge and stitch to front arm. Tension fabric to back and tack.

To position outside arm fabric so pattern aligns, temporarily tack bottom edge to underside of bottom rail, matching pattern to front arm. Pin mark where fabric meets underarm at front and back, remove temporary tacks and reposition on underarm so the front pin is the width of the back tack strip from the outer edge of the back tack strip. This allows for folding the fabric over the strip and into the corner. The back pin and outer edge of back tack strip should align with outside edge of back upright at back of arm.

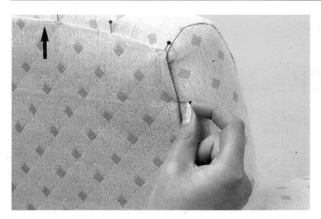

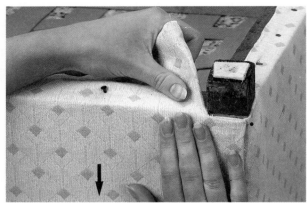

24 Centre outside back fabric on back of chair and pin to back, tucking edges under. Tension by temporarily tacking to underside of bottom rail. Stitch in place.

25 Turn chair upside down and make a diagonal cut to inside back corner of uprights. Tuck fabric under, pin and stitch at back, and tack to rail at side of leg.

26 Cut hessian slightly larger than underside of chair and temporarily tack to opposite rails, turning edges under. Fit round legs as before and complete tacking.

To fit the arm fabric over the bottom back rail, fold diagonally, make a diagonal cut towards the rail, and then a smaller slanting cut, as shown. Turn under the long edges, leaving the V-shaped flap on top of the rail. To fit foam round front seat rail, turn foam back so fold meets edge of arm, then remove a rectangle the width of the front seat rail, cutting to within 2.5cm of fold. Turn foam down around sides of chair and trim front to butt up against edge of front facing.

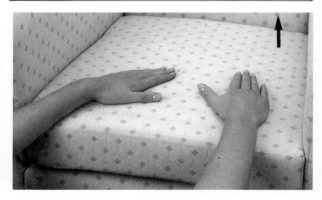

27 Make up the gusseted cushion cover as for a simple box cushion without piping. Taking the zip round the sides of the cushion makes it easier to insert the pad.

28 Insert the foam cushion pad into the cover and arrange the seams so they sit on the edge of the cushion. Fit into the covered seat of the chair and press down firmly.

Making a deep-buttoned headboard

A deep-buttoned headboard gives luxury and comfort to a bed, and by upholstering your own you can choose a fabric to co-ordinate with your room. Headboards can be made to any shape or size to fit your bed. The pattern and instructions given here are for a 90cm single headboard cut from either chipboard or blockboard with a slightly curved top edge. To re-cover an existing headboard, follow these instructions, providing that the shape is not too ornate. Check the overall size, and if necessary, adjust the button positions. Extend or reduce the rows of diamonds to fit the new shape, allowing a border of about 8cm around the buttoned area.

Making your own luxurious deep-buttoned headboard is surprisingly easy.

Materials guide

Chipboard or blockboard: These are both fairly inexpensive substitutes for solid wood, and are easy to obtain. Either of these materials would make a firm base for the headboard and both have good smooth surfaces for attaching the foam padding. Choose a good-quality 12mm chipboard, or blockboard. Most local timber merchants will cut your headboard for you from a paper pattern drawn to actual size.

Standard 5cm × 1.5cm white wood: This is used for the two supports attached to the back of the headboard and to the base of the bed.

Foam padding: This may be made from latex or polyether in different thicknesses (5cm is best here) and degrees of hardness. Seating quality will give a firm headboard, although less dense qualities are perfectly adequate. Foam is used in place of traditional fillings which are more difficult to use. Local suppliers will usually cut foam to a given pattern.

Cotton wadding: This is 46cm-wide 'super white' quality. It covers the foam to protect it from light, which can cause it to disintegrate. It also gives a softer finish to the upholstery.

Calico: This will cover the wadding and makes a permanent undercover to the upholstery. Unbleached calico comes in wide widths and different weights. Choose light-weight for deep buttoning.

Upholstery fabric: Ideal for the top cover. It should be closely woven, and preferably spongeable. Pile fabrics, such as synthetic velvets, can be successfully used with the pile running across the headboard. Plain or small patterned fabrics are best.

Lining: Covers the raw fabric edges and tacks at the back of the headboard to give a neat finish. For light-coloured upholstery, choose best-quality matching curtain lining, and for dark top fabrics, use upholsterer's lining. This is available in 80cm and 122cm widths.

Buttons: These can be covered by hand, using button moulds or two-part clips. Alternatively, many large stores operate a button-covering service.

Upholsterer's tacks: These are specially made with needle-sharp points which respond easily to thumb pressure.

Upholsterer's hammers: These are not essential but because they are light and specially balanced, they are easier for most people to handle. The magnetic type picks up the tack by the head, ready for tapping in.

Regulators: These are used to neaten the pleats formed by the buttonwork. Use the flat ends.

Buttoning needles: These are straight, double-ended needles. You will need a 20cm or 25cm needle.

How to make your headboard

WHAT YOU NEED

1 12mm-thick chipboard or blockboard
2 Two pieces wood 70cm × 5cm × 1.5cm
3 5cm-thick foam padding
4 Cotton wadding
5 Calico for undercover and strips
6 Cover fabric
7 Lining
8 Sixteen 15mm self-covered buttons
9 10mm and 15mm improved tacks
10 Upholsterer's hammer
11 Two regulators (or flat lolly sticks)

12 20cm straight buttoning needle
13 No 2 button twine
14 Back tack strip or thin strips of card
15 Oddments of webbing for toggles
16 Latex fabric adhesive
17 Drill, 4mm, 5mm and 12mm bits
18 Four 38mm No 8 screws and cups
19 Bradawl
20 Jigsaw or general-purpose DIY saw
Plus: Cutting-out scissors, pencil, ruler,
large sheet of brown paper, screwdrivers

How to work out your quantities

Chipboard or blockboard: Measure the width of your bed. For a 90cm-wide bed, transfer the pattern on to brown paper.
Foam: Make a pattern following the measurements given, allowing 1.5cm extra at top and sides.
Cotton wadding: Use pattern for foam and add 12cm to top and side edges, plus 8cm to bottom edge. Also allow the width and depth of the unpadded section.
Calico: Using paper pattern, add 3.5cm

in both directions for each diamond, plus 12cm for turnings at the top and two sides, and 10cm at bottom edge. Allow extra for 10cm-wide strips, each the length of one side of foam, plus 15cm.
Top fabric: Calculate as for calico, adding 3cm in both directions for each diamond. For bottom section, allow the width of the headboard, plus 12cm for turnings, and the depth of the unpadded section plus 10cm.
Lining: Use headboard pattern.

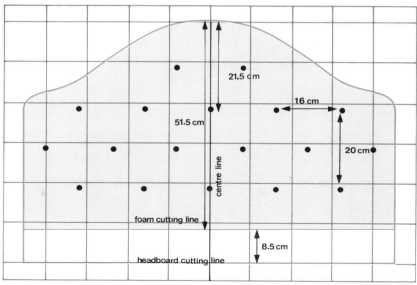

21.5 cm

16 cm

51.5 cm

centre line

20 cm

foam cutting line

headboard cutting line

8.5 cm

1 square = 10 cm

To enlarge the pattern, draw a grid of 10cm squares on brown paper and copy the outline given for half the shape, up to the centre line. Fold in half and cut out to obtain a symmetrical pattern. Cut chipboard to shape and mark centre line, foam cutting line, then button positions.

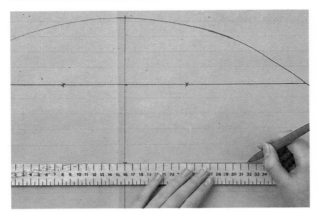

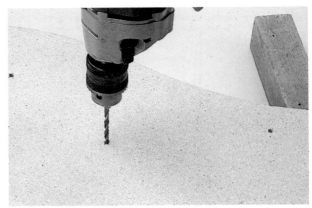

1 To make the button pattern, lay the cut chipboard shape on paper and draw round edge. Mark foam cutting line and centre line. Measure button positions out from the centre.

2 Align paper pattern on chipboard shape and mark each button position on board by piercing the paper with a sharp pencil. Check the positions and drill holes using a 5mm bit.

3 Cut foam to shape. Using cutting-out scissors, bevel the edges on one side of the foam by trimming off 25mm-wide strips, angling the scissors to give a diagonal cut.

4 Fold each calico strip in half lengthwise and stick one half to the uncut perimeter of the foam. For correct positioning, match foldline with the edge of the foam. Allow to dry.

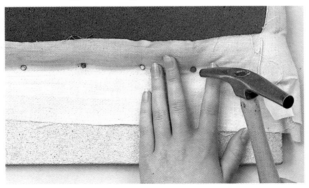

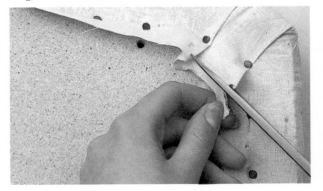

5 Place foam on chipboard, aligning bottom edge with foam cutting line. Pull calico down on to board and tack through calico and foam with 10mm tacks, working from centre out.

6 Tack remaining strips to back of board, pulling the calico taut to roll the edge of the foam over the edge of the chipboard. Pleat corners to neaten and trim excess calico.

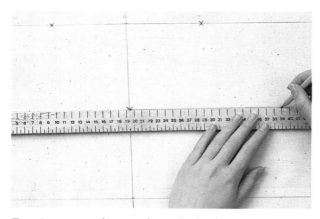

7 Cut out calico and mark the button positions, measuring out from the centre. To allow for pleats, add 35mm to original distances between buttons in each direction.

8 Cover the foam with a layer of cotton wadding and then position the calico on top, matching the centre line on the calico with the centre line on the board.

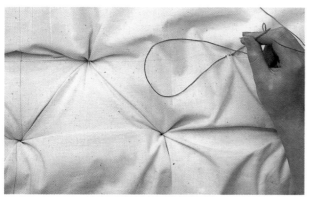

9 Thread a buttoning needle with a long length of twine. Working from the back, push it right up through each drilled hole and take back again, leaving long thread ends.

10 Cut 2cm squares of webbing and roll up to make temporary toggles. Fasten thread ends over the toggles with a slip knot. Pull tight to draw in the foam.

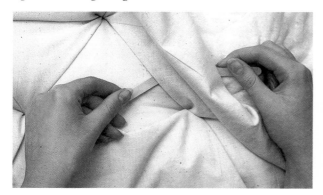

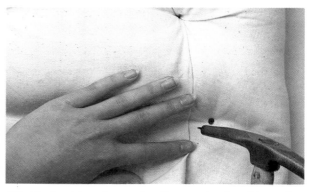

11 Once two rows are worked, neaten the pleats by working a regulator or lolly stick up and down each of the pleat's folds. Continue making pleats with each row worked.

12 Tack side edges of calico to back of board, then form pleats round outer edges. Arrange pleats vertically at lower edge and diagonally at top edge to continue the pattern.

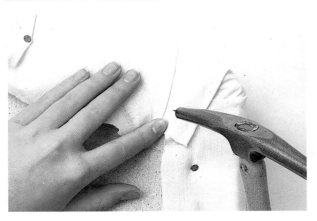

13 Once the pleats are tacked in place, finish tacking the edges of the calico to the back of the board to hold secure. Make neat corners by folding carefully and pleating.

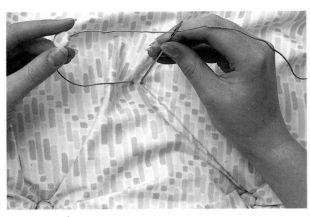

14 Mark button positions on wrong side of top fabric, adding 3cm to the original distances between buttons. Attach as calico, threading on buttons and pleating as you go.

15 To secure buttons permanently, tack each side of toggles with 13mm tacks, and remove toggle and first set of twine. Wind thread round tacks, hammer in and trim.

16 Check pleats on front of headboard, then finish pleating at the outer edge as with the calico. Tack lower edge to front of board and top and sides to the back.

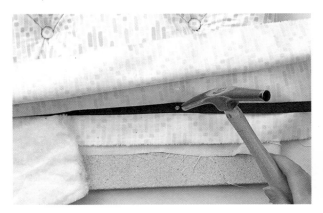

17 Cut a piece of back tack strip slightly longer than the width of the board. Place lower section of top fabric right side down and secure invisibly by tacking. Add wadding.

18 Turn lower section of top fabric to the back of the board and tack in place. Cut out a rectangle of fabric slightly narrower than the turning and fold neatly to mitre.

19 Cut lining to size of headboard and turn under seam allowances all round, leaving the lining big enough to cover all previous tacks. Tack to back of board.

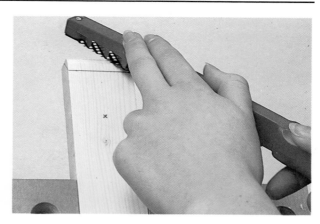

20 Mark positions for screw holes 4.5cm and 14.5cm from one end of each upright. Bevel the corner, taking off 1cm from top edge, and drill holes with a 4mm bit.

21 Drill a hole at the centre of each upright, 25cm from the opposite end, using a 12mm bit. Draw parallel lines to the end of the upright and saw a slot with a jigsaw or handsaw.

22 Position the headboard on bed with the uprights on the bolts to find where they need to be screwed to the headboard. Make preparatory holes with a bradawl.

23 Screw the uprights to the back of the headboard, using 38mm No 8 chipboard screws and cups to give a neat finish. Screw in tight to hold secure.

24 Position the headboard on the bed with the uprights over the bolts, so bottom of padded section sits on the top of the mattress. Tighten the bolts to hold in place.

CHAPTER 4

Cleaning & Repairing

Once you have created your ideal home it is best to establish a simple routine to help you keep it that way. Tiresome stains can be removed from fabrics by consulting our quick reference list at the beginning of the chapter, and we show you how to care for household metals, making them a shining asset to your home. In a section on repairing and cleaning wall coverings we show you how to repair parting seams, attend to air bubbles and patch damaged wallpaper, removing stains as you go. Lengthening the life of your carpet is always worthwhile. The step-by-step instructions tell you how to disguise burn marks, patch worn areas and fit threshold strips as well as how to spread wear on the stairs. Don't despair if you break your favourite piece of china. This chapter has repair hints that will make it look as good as new.

Removing stains from fabrics

There are some furnishing fabrics from which it is more difficult to remove stains than others. Most are featured here with different stains to show you how to deal with a variety of accidents.

Know your fabric

Without care labels and with over 200 fibre blends, only a textile chemist is equipped to identify today's furnishing fabrics accurately. Ready-made loose covers, curtains and bedding bearing care labels denoting fibre content and washability can in many cases be considered for DIY spot removal. However, those items marked 'dry clean only' should not be treated at home. Stains on fabrics with flame- or water-resistant finishes and those that are not colour-fast, should be given to the dry cleaners. Certain cleaning chemicals and temperatures can also cause problems with acetates, acrylics and nylon nets. Home-made soft furnishing items will not have convenient care labels attached, so keep some spare pieces for making spot removal experiments. Note the fibre content often printed on the selvedge edge.

Know your stain

Speed is of the essence in all stain removal. Decide whether your stain is solvent or water-based: use water for water-based stains, solvent spirit for spirit-based ones. Except in rare cases, heat should never be applied either by water or ironing as it sets stains irretrievably.

Your stain removal kit

Chemicals used in DIY stain removal can be dangerous; toxic fumes are a health hazard so always work in well-ventilated rooms or, better still, outdoors. Many cleaning chemicals can instantly dissolve plastic and rubber and corrode metal so check you have a supply of old wooden spoons and ceramic or glass bowls for mixing. Do not work near a naked flame or smoke as these chemicals are also highly flammable. Keep all chemicals well out of children's reach; never put cleaning chemicals in old lemonade bottles.

Branded stain removers are usually the most convenient way of buying chemicals that are difficult to obtain over the counter. As there is no such thing as a universal all-purpose stain remover, you can expect to stock quite a few. For example, carbon tetrachloride is found in many grease and tar-removing products; amyl acetate (banana oil) is often the main ingredient of cellulose paint thinners (never use it on acetates). It is difficult to obtain from chemists in small amounts. Acetone can be substituted instead, but is less effective although easily obtainable as nail polish remover. Colour-free methylated spirits (methyl alcohol) is also a useful solvent for some ball point and felt pen stains, whereas ordinary methylated spirit with its violet aniline dye can sometimes stain white and delicate fabrics. Oxalic acid used for rust and iron mould stains is highly toxic and can be harsh on old fabrics. Buy a branded product.

The most convenient stain removers are cleaning chemicals already found in the home. Certain paint brush cleaners for instance make a useful solvent for many grease stains, and are particularly effective when used with washing-up liquid. They should not come in contact with plastic or rubber. Biological pre-washes are excellent pre-soak remedies for a number of protein and animal-based stains such as milk, blood, egg, etc, but water mustn't be hotter than 60°C or enzyme action is impaired. There may also be colour loss on non-fast fabrics. Washing-up liquid, liquid detergents and ordinary household bar soaps are also helpful on furnishing fabric stains, particularly in dealing with leftover sugar, grease or dye residues after using solvent cleaners. Eucalyptus oil is another traditional remedy for treating all kinds of grease and tar stains and is useful for treating sun-tan oil and curry. Another important aid is laundry borax (sodium pyrobate) which is invaluable for grease and wine stains on cottons.

Bleaches are also useful to whiten and deodorise fabrics. Ordinary domestic bleach (sodium hypochlorite) is fine for cottons, but use hydrogen peroxide which is a more delicate oxygen bleach, normally sold in a 9 or 20 volume solution for home use on wool or silk. Ammonia, too, is a useful alkali for removing dirt and grease and is sold as a 10% solution in DIY shops.

Fabrics stain removal chart

A

Adhesives

Any kind of adhesive is more difficult to remove when set; old stains should always be taken to the dry cleaners. Do not try to remove adhesives from towelling and pile fabrics, i.e. velvet. Try to work from the back of adhesive-stained fabrics; textured weaves and fitted upholstery can be treated from fabric's right side. The following treatments are suitable for washable fabrics: **Clear household** As shown on page 120. **Contact adhesives** First try methylated spirit, then amyl acetate. Do not use either solvent on acetates or triacetates. **Epoxy resin** If still soft try methylated spirit; if hard take straight to dry cleaners. **Latex** Manufacturers can supply a special solvent; otherwise try a brush cleaner and restorer. **PVA wood glues** When still wet, remove excess with wet cloth, then apply neat washing-up liquid before washing according to fabric. **Superglue** Act immediately, saturate cleaning pad with water and hold on area until glue loosens. Do not attempt this on napped fabric or the surface will be ruined.

Alcohol

Perfume stains also come under this heading. Never delay over stain removal. **Champagne** Can oxidise on fabrics if left for even a short time. Stains turn bright yellow. Cottons, and linen unions etc should be washed in warm sudsy water then washed at highest temperature. **Cider/lager** On washable fabrics, mop up excess liquid with kitchen paper, sponge with sudsy water. Or soak items in cold water, then wash according to fabric, at hottest temperature. **Perfume** Soak washable fabrics immediately in warm sudsy water. Take dried-in stains on all fabrics (including washable ones) to dry cleaners. **White/red wine stains** As shown on page 123. Do not try diluting red wine stains with white as this can set stain more. Take non-washable fabrics to dry cleaners, and tell them what caused the stain in the first place.

Animal stains See Biological.

B

Ballpoint See Ink.

Beer See Alcohol, lager.

Biological/Animal

Protein stains blood, milk, egg yolk, gravy etc, on washable cottons and linens (colourfast). Soak overnight in biological detergent. Repeat if stains persist. Send woollen blankets, loose covers etc, to dry cleaners. **Excreta** On washable fabrics, scrape off any deposits with blunt knife. Rinse well under running cold water. Soak white cotton and linen in a solution of bleach— 1 eggcupful to 1 gallon of cold water—for 2–3 hours. Launder in heavy duty detergent. Non-washable fabrics, treat with pads of absorbent kitchen paper, cold water and ammonia solution: 1 part ammonia to 3 parts water. Blot excess and take straight to dry cleaners. **Urine** Blot up excess with absorbent kitchen roll. Then rinse in cold running water. Soak white cottons in bleach solution (see Excreta), then launder in heavy duty detergent. Take non-washable fabrics to the dry cleaners after rinsing and blotting excess water. **Vomit** Scrape off surface deposits with blunt knife or spoon. Rinse well in cold running water. Soak white cottons (see Excreta), then wash in heavy duty detergent. For wool and for fitted upholstery, sponge with absorbent kitchen paper and solution of vinegar: 1 cupful to 1 pint of water. Blot, then take to dry cleaners, or call in expert in situ cleaning firm.

Bleach

Stains by most bleaches cause immediate colour-loss from non-fast dyed fabrics. Either re-dye the same colour if fabric can be dyed, or camouflage small marks on cotton and linen union prints with fabric paints.

Butter See Grease.

C

Candlewax

One of the few times heat is applied. Pick or scrape off excess with blunt knife or fingernail. Then sandwich stained area between two sheets of absorbent kitchen paper and press with a warm iron. Change paper every time wax is absorbed. Use a grease solvent on residues then wash as

117

normal. For upholstery, place absorbent paper on fabric and press. Wipe off residues with a grease solvent then treat with a little upholstery shampoo. Sponge with clear water and blot dry with absorbent paper.

Champagne See Alcohol.

Chewing/Bubblegum/Plasticine/Putty
Pick off any excess beforehand. Treat small amounts with solvent cleaner. Alternatively put ice cubes in a plastic bag and hold against gum to harden then pick off. (Do not use this last method on pile fabrics, these should be taken to the dry cleaners.)

Chocolates/Soft sweets As shown on page 121.

Cocoa See Coffee/tea.

Cod Liver Oil See Medicines.

Coffee/Tea/Cocoa
As shown on page 122. Non-washable fabrics should be dry cleaned. Duvets may well need special treatment from manufacturers as fillings may be affected. PVC fabrics stained on non-laminated side may respond to sponging with biological powder solution and warm water if treated immediately. Cocoa dye residues can be treated with methylated spirit.

Cough Mixture See Medicines.

Cream See Grease.

Curry
It is the turmeric in curry that leaves such a persistent yellow stain on table linen; it is a vegetable dye that can be very difficult to remove. For non-washable fabrics, dry cleaners suggest treating mishaps with a drop of olive oil or eucalyptus oil as this suspends dye colour. Items should then be taken in for dry cleaning. White table linen can be treated with neat washing-up liquid and then spot treated with a proprietary dye remover. Finish by soaking in a fabric brightener.

D

Dyes-Fabric/Henna and Hair Colourants
Dye colours on white, washable fabrics can be treated with a proprietary dye remover, but do not use on non-colour fast fabrics. Henna and other hair colourants can leave stains on household furnishings. These usually wash out if treated to overnight soaking in detergent; heavier stains may need bleaching: 1 eggcupful to 1 gallon. Wash in heavy duty detergent. Henna acts as a bleach on non-fast deep dyed articles, see Bleach for suggested remedies. For henna stains on white woollen fabrics use hydrogen peroxide in a 20 vol solution: 1 part to 4 parts water.

E

Egg See Biological

F

Felt-tip pens See Ink.

Fruit/Vegetable
Worst culprits are fruit squash and lollipop stains on non-washable fabrics. These can disappear into light coloured loose covers, only to reappear after dry cleaning as untreatable 'caramelized' brown stains. For washable fabrics, soak overnight in a branded product of fabric brightener. Work neat washing-up liquid or detergent into remaining residues and wash according to fabric.

Furniture polish
Misfiring with aerosol sprays can cause mishaps to upholstery and curtains. Work in neat washing-up liquid and wash out. For thicker, greasy polishes, scrape off excess with a knife, then treat with washing-up liquid massaging well into fabric, wash out blotting up excess moisture with absorbent kitchen paper. Non-washable fabrics should be taken to the dry cleaners.

G

Glue See Adhesives.

Grass
Try a saturated pad of methylated spirit on the wrong side of fabric pushing out stain the way it came in. Small grass stains on white fitted upholstery and furnishing fabrics may respond to a branded product paste cleaner.

Gravy See Biological.

Grease/Oils/Boot polish
Treat heavy stains on washable fabrics with a solvent-based cleaner containing carbon tetrachloride, then wash in heavy detergent at hottest temperature fabric can take. For upholstery, a paste dry cleaner can be used for small grease stains on white fabrics; heavily ingrained areas and pile fabrics may need professional cleaning.

H

Hair lacquer
Treat fabric first with a cotton pad soaked in acetone or amyl acetate.

Honey See Jams.

I

Ink
You must identify the type of ink as wrong treatment can set stains irretrievably. Small recent stains can sometimes be treated on washable fabrics, but all others including old ink stains should be taken to the dry cleaners. **Ballpoint** Saturate pad with methylated spirit or proprietary brand of ballpoint pen remover. Wash in warm sudsy water. Take stubborn stains and those on washable fabrics to the dry cleaners. **Felt tip pens** Water-soluble stains can be held under running cold water until most of the colour has gone, then wash as usual. Others respond to blotting and pressure with a pad of methylated spirit or branded removal product. Treat residues with liquid detergent, working this well in to fabric. **Permanent ink** Seek professional advice. **Washable ink** Recent stains on washable cottons can sometimes be sponged out with cold water before washing in heavy duty detergent. Small brown marks can then be treated as for rust and iron mould.

Iron Mould See Rust.

J

Jam/Marmalade/Honey/Syrup
For washable fabrics, scrape off excess with blunt knife, then blot with absorbent kitchen paper. Apply neat washing-up liquid or liquid detergent, massaging well into fabric. Rinse out in cold water and launder according to fabric. Non-washable fabrics must be dry cleaned.

L

Lipstick See Make-up.

M

Make-up
On washable fabrics, remove surplus with blunt knife. Treat with solvent cleaner. Massage any residues with liquid detergent or washing-up liquid. Before this dries, launder in heavy duty detergent.

Mayonnaise
On washable fabrics, scrape off excess with blunt knife then treat with neat washing-up liquid. Alternatively soak overnight in a biological detergent.

Metal polish
On washable fabrics, dab with pad saturated in white spirit. When dry use a soft brush to remove powdery residues. Launder in heavy duty detergent according to fabric. For upholstery, seek professional advice.

Mildew
If recent, wash in heavy duty detergent. Dry out in strong sunlight. Soak white cotton and linen fabrics in bleach solution—1 tablespoon to 2 pts of water—then wash. Marks usually disappear with repeated laundering.

Milk See Biological.

Mud
On washable fabrics, allow to dry out thoroughly before brushing out; treat stubborn residues with neat washing-up liquid, then wash according to fabric.

Mustard See Jam.

N

Nail polish See Paint: cellulose.

Newsprint See Grease.

O

Oils See Grease.

Orange Juice See Fruit.

P

Paint
Unless treated instantly, most paints will need professional stain removal once they have dried hard whether fabrics are washable or dry clean only. Never try and remove paint from pile fabrics. Different paints require stain removal treatments as follows: **Cellulose modelling paints, nail polishes** Try acetone or amyl acetate. (Do not use on acetates or triacetates.) **Emulsion (acrylic)** Try dabbing with a little methylated spirit while still wet. Take dried stains to drycleaners. **Gloss and oil paint** If still wet, try blotting with a pad saturated with a solvent cleaner. Do not wash or stain may set. **Polyurethane varnish** Try white spirit on wet stains, then liquid detergent and launder as normal.

119

Perfume See Alcohol.

Plasticine See Chewing gum.

Polish See Metal polish and Grease.

Putty See Chewing gum.

R

Rust
Stains are caused by metal fastenings; clogged up steam irons can also spatter rust. On white washable fabrics, recent stains may respond to painting with diluted citric acid dissolved in a little water. Failing that, use a proprietary rust remover. As shown on page 124, the traditional method is to use a diluted solution of oxalic acid in a 3% solution, painting this on offending areas. Do not leave longer than 10 minutes or fabric may disintegrate. Oxalic acid is highly toxic and any remaining solution should be disposed of down w.c. Wear rubber gloves when using and a ceramic or glass bowl for mixing as metal corrodes. To prevent rust mould stains reappearing, rinse items thoroughly after treatment in purified water, which is available from large chemists.

S

Scorch marks
Nothing can be done about heavy scorch marks. Light ones on white wool can be treated with diluted hydrogen peroxide. Seek expert advice over cigarette burns, as some dry cleaners can arrange invisible mending or reweaving.

Shoe polish See Grease.

Sun tan oil As shown on page 123.

T

Tar As shown on page 124.

Tea See Coffee.

U

Urine See Biological.

V

Vomit See Biological.

W

Wax polish See Grease.

Wine See Alcohol.

Adhesive

Here, a clear household adhesive was left to harden on a light cotton textured weave fabric cushion cover. Not only had the adhesive adhered to the fabric but to the cushion below, which meant treating the fabric as fixed upholstery.

When dealing with blobs of hardened adhesive, you could damage the fibre by trying to scrape it off, so use the recommended solvent to soften and loosen the adhesive, then remove it with a clean cloth.

> **WHAT YOU NEED**
> Amyl acetate or nail
>   polish remover
> Cotton wool
> Clean sheeting

1 Make sure the fabric can be treated with a solvent cleaner. Look for a care label and carry out a test.

2 Apply a little amyl acetate on a pad of lint-free cotton, and press down hard on to fabric to lift out stain.

You may need to change the pad several times before stain disappears, so be prepared to spend some time working on it.

Biro

Any type of ink stain, whether biro, felt-tip, ballpoint, washable or permanent, must first be definitely identified before stain removal treatments are carried out. If the stains are on non-washable fabrics, then make sure you use the right solvent cleaners and that you don't over-soak any fixed fabrics.

Plasticized materials, like PVC, need to be treated carefully as the solvent cleaner will often affect the finish.

Here, we show how a typical biro stain was successfully removed with methylated spirits and washing-up liquid.

| WHAT YOU NEED |
| Methylated spirits |
| Clean white sheeting |
| Washing-up liquid |

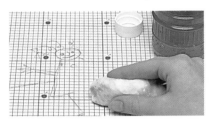

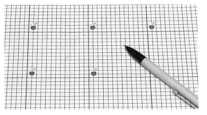

1 Screw a small piece of lint-free sheeting into a pad. Apply a little methylated spirits and rub into stain.

2 If there is still a faint blur on the PVC, often a little neat washing-up liquid rubbed in will remove any residues.

Any lingering smell of methylated spirits should disappear very quickly, but if not, leave outside for a time.

Chocolate

With any food stains, like chocolate or sweets, you must first remove the residues, then tackle the stain itself which may have seeped into the fabric. Often discovered when it has hardened on to the fabric, the stain has inevitably spread. Identify the food stain first, then your fabric and then treat. If the fabric has a nap or pile, like velvet, there are additional problems in removing the stain without causing damage to the pile.

Chocolate stains will need to be treated differently depending on whether they are on washable or 'dry clean only' fabrics.

| WHAT YOU NEED |
| Blunt knife |
| Solvent spot remover |
| White cloth |
| Fine toothbrush |

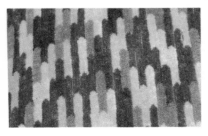

1 Test first, apply a little cleaner on a pad of cloth, dabbing rather than rubbing to avoid spreading stain.

2 Before the fabric dries, use a fine toothbrush to gently brush the nap back into position, working with nap.

Sometimes even the most careful stain removal can leave tiny holes. This cannot be avoided on this type of fabric.

Coffee

An occupational hazard when having breakfast in bed or a warm bedtime drink is tea, coffee and cocoa stains on the bedding.

If treated immediately, the stains will usually respond to a good soak in a solution of pre-wash biological powder, if the fabric is washable.

Immediately the accident occurs, prevent the stain spreading underneath by soaking up with pads of clean white tissues. Biological pre-wash powders can cause skin irritation, so always use protective rubber gloves, and avoid inhaling the powder fumes.

WHAT YOU NEED
Plastic bucket
Biological pre-wash
  powder
Wooden spoon
Rubber gloves

1 If the item is quite small, like this pillowcase, mix up a solution of pre-wash powder and warm water in a bucket.

2 Drop stained fabric, making sure the stain lies below the water line and leave for the specified time.

Don't leave the bedding in any longer than the time recommended. Follow with a normal warm wash.

Lipstick

Lipstick is a grease-based stain and therefore requires a solvent formulation to remove it from all types of fabric—for details of how to remove lipstick from washable fabrics, see page 119.

First remove as much of the residue as you can. Do this with a blunt knife, but avoid spreading the stain.

Certain proprietary paint brush cleaners work well on this type of grease stain, but always carry out a test first. Hold absorbent towels above and below the stained area.

WHAT YOU NEED
White absorbent
  kitchen towels
Proprietary brush
  cleaner solvent
White cotton wool
Washing-up liquid

1 Lay absorbent kitchen towels on to a flat surface, then the stained napkin on top. Apply solvent cleaner.

2 When most of the stain has been removed, rub neat washing-up liquid into this area with your fingers.

Once you are satisfied that the traces of lipstick have gone, you can follow your normal washing procedure.

Oil

This type of stain not only stains quickly but it sinks well into the fabric if left. As a solvent cleaner is required to lift out the stain, be careful to check that it is compatible with the fabric being treated. For details of oil and grease stain treatments, see page 118.

You can use proprietary grease removers that will be successful with difficult stains, but try eucalyptus oil first.

The deckchair canvas featured here was splashed with suntan oil, and found not to be colour-fast. Where fabric is cleaned in situ, rub a little washing-up liquid into stain and clean off with a cloth.

> ## WHAT YOU NEED
> **White kitchen towels**
> **Cotton wool buds (white)**
> **Eucalyptus oil**
> **Washing-up liquid**

1 To avoid spreading stain, lightly dab eucalyptus oil round outside of stain and work inwards to the centre.

2 Now place an absorbent pad of kitchen towels underneath stain, and press down firmly.

It may take a number of treatments to take out the oil stain. Be careful that the colour doesn't run.

Red Wine

This is much more difficult to remove than white wine as the fruit juice quickly stains and sinks into the fabric unless treated immediately.

There are many old-fashioned remedies for treating wine stains, but the real secret is to apply plenty of absorbent tissues to the stain immediately to soak up the liquid.

Here we show you how to cope with a red wine accident on a linen table-cloth by immediately neutralizing the acid in the wine with ordinary household salt.

> ## WHAT YOU NEED
> **White tissues**
> **Household salt**
> **Laundry borax**
> **Wooden spoon**
> **Bucket**

1 Immediately stain occurs, place white tissues underneath, and sprinkle on plenty of salt.

2 Mix 1 tablespoon borax with 1 pint warm water in plastic bucket. Soak fabric until stain disappears.

You can also treat white cotton and linen with household bleach, but protect your hands and follow instructions.

Rust

Rust or iron mould is a particular hazard of the DIY-er, who may be cleaning a bike or moving rusty tools in a shed. But rust can also be found on materials that are left for a long time in an airing cupboard. Linens are particularly prone to rust marks. Here we show how to remove them from this type of natural fabric.

An old remedy is to use lemon juice. Better still, is a special formulation bought in the form of a proprietary product. Less dangerous than oxalic acid, it will also be easier on weak old linen.

1 Dampen the stain with plenty of cold water applied on a pad of clean cloth. Place kitchen towels underneath.

2 Sprinkle stain with proprietary powder and leave for 5–10 minutes. Rinse with luke-warm water. Repeat.

If the linen is a little dingy through age, brighten it up with a proprietary whitening agent prior to washing.

Tar

Tar can be very difficult to remove from those fabrics with particularly long piles, like towels, which often get stained when used on the beach. These steps show you how to remove the stain from a coloured 100% cotton beach towel, without damaging the fibres.

Before you attempt to tackle the stain itself, always try to take off as much of the tar as you can by using a blunt knife to scrape it off. When the blade becomes sticky, wipe off, before re-applying to the fabric. To avoid the stain spreading, isolate by tying with string.

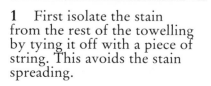

1 First isolate the stain from the rest of the towelling by tying it off with a piece of string. This avoids the stain spreading.

2 Pour liquid into china bowl, dip in stained area for a few minutes, repeat if necessary changing the liquid each time.

A hot wash with a detergent powder will take out any residue, but make sure that there is only a faint mark left.

Caring for everyday metals

Many household items, practical, ornamental or both, are wholly or in part made of metal. Knowing why some are used on their own while others are combined—and how to recognize the various metals—is relevant to their proper care.

How metals are produced
Pure metals are those strong enough, and attractive enough, to be used on their own. Gold, silver, copper and iron are the main ones, but there are other, lesser-known pure metals, such as antimony, zinc and chromium.

Alloys are a mixture of metals—mixed together in varying proportions for economy, strength or beauty. Bronze is the oldest alloy used by man. Originally, it was made from copper and tin, though other metals have been—

and still are—added. Brass and pewter are other common alloys.

Plated ware is another category of metal—in which a thin coating of one metal is placed on another. Examples of plating are Sheffield plate (silver on copper), EPNS (electroplate on nickel silver) and Britannia metal (silver on an alloy of copper, antimony and tin). Silver and gold will be dealt with in a later chapter.

Identifying your metal
When they are dirty and corroded, it is hard to

If the finish is carefully restored, old, badly tarnished metalware will reward you with a soft glow. Regular cleaning will then preserve its looks.

identify metals. Try rubbing a small, inconspicuous area with cleaning abrasive on a cloth to reveal the true surface of the metal. Then check this against other items you have identified.

Simple renovation

Nearly all forms of tarnish and corrosion are caused by oxidization, that is, the action on the metal of oxygen in the air, combined with impurities such as smoke or petrol and diesel fumes or salt from sea air.

Moisture is another enemy of metal, and discolouration can be caused by some timbers, such as oak (so collector's coins should not be stored in an oak cabinet). Corrosion is a much more

serious deterioration—caused by some household paints and fruit juices left in metal dishes.

Approach cleaning with due caution, for while most materials deteriorate if neglected, over-cleaning or careless cleaning can ruin a piece; never disturb the patina of an antique metal piece. And remember that each time an item is cleaned, a minute fraction of the surface is removed. If in doubt about the advisability of cleaning ask for professional advice from a large city museum.

Safety precautions

There are so many excellent and safe products on the market for cleaning metal, that it is unneces-

Identifying metals

Brass

Ancient brass was an alloy of copper and tin but modern brass is often copper and zinc with, perhaps, other metals added. By the 1800s, brass casting was being used for decorative objects and architectural ornament.

The quality of brass varies according to the proportions of the alloy. No amount of rubbing can give a brilliant shine to poor quality brass. It is recognizable by its bright yellow surface, which can be light or dark depending on its condition and composition.

Pewter

Pewter is an alloy of tin, copper and antimony, widely used in Europe since the Middle Ages for domestic utensils and ornaments.

It does not rust but does darken with age and then it needs a good clean. Recognized by its grey appearance, it is usually left with a dull sheen. Sometimes it is highly polished to look like silver, but always looks darker.

Pewter is a light-weight metal and this helps to distinguish it from silver, which is heavier.

Copper

Copper is the oldest natural metal known to man, dating back to the European bronze age. Its malleable quality made it ideal for cooking pots and other domestic ware, though it was not known for many years that food poisoning could result from cooking certain foods in copper pans. These are therefore now lined with other metals, such as aluminium.

Easily recognized by its attractive, warm pink-red colour, copper polishes brightly. All these characteristics make it sought after by collectors.

sary to mix up your own potentially dangerous chemicals. Paint stripper or cellulose thinners will remove old lacquer finish, rust removers will remove corrosion on brass as well as rust on iron, and car cleaning abrasive will not scratch the surface. Do not use household cleaners or coarse sandpapers.

Protect your hands with rubber or PVC gloves while cleaning. Wear cotton gloves when handling a cleaned item if it is to be lacquered or try to avoid touching the metal; fingerprints can prevent the lacquer from adhering.

Protect the surface of metals from accidental scratches caused by small particles of grit or dust: place the metal on a clean soft cloth or mat of plastic foam, on the table on which you are working.

After-cleaning protection
Unlacquered metals, kept in a city atmosphere, need routine cleaning about every two weeks. Lacquered metals will last up to a year, depending on the amount of exposure to the elements.

Lacquering has no effect on the value of the items. Buy a good quality proprietary brand for the best result. As an alternative to lacquering, if the metal is not to have much handling, give it a protective coating of wax furniture polish after cleaning. This method of protection is suitable for metals like pewter, iron and steel.

Iron
Iron is an important base metal. Hard and tough, it can be heated to a molten temperature, then poured into castings, or hammered into shape (wrought iron). It has been used for tools, weapons and domestic items especially those associated with fires and fireplaces. In its heyday wrought iron was much used for balconies, external staircases and railings.

Iron's great disadvantage is that it rusts badly. Recognized by its heavy weight and dull black surface.

Steel
Steel is an iron-carbon alloy, so widely used that without it our civilization could hardly exist as we know it. Before modern technology made it possible to treat steel to make it stainless, ordinary steel was as rust prone as iron but it was still used for bridges and industrial undertakings, as well as for fire irons, fenders, knives and other domestic items.

It is difficult to distinguish steel from iron when they are rusty, but steel is wrought, not cast and will polish to quite a bright surface.

Aluminium
Aluminium, another base metal, was hailed as the wonder metal of the day when it was discovered around the middle of the 19th century. Light and durable, it was at one time thought that it would supersede gold and silver.

Used mainly for aircraft, industrial and building purposes and for everyday kitchen items where its heat conducting properties are useful, aluminium is resistant to corrosion.

This metal often resembles stainless steel or chromium but is lighter and paler in colour. It is usually left matt.

These traditional household items have been carefully restored, and if properly looked after they will last for generations.

Brass and copper

If there are signs of active corrosion on valuable brass and copper, consult the conservation department of your local museum before renovating as below or using the time-honoured method of salt and vinegar, or the juice of half a lemon and salt, applied on a stiff brush. Wash off and polish.

For regular cleaning rub over about once a fortnight with impregnated wadding and gently buff with a clean cloth.

WHAT YOU NEED
Rust remover, Brushes
Wadding, 000 steel wool

1 Wear rubber gloves and gently brush the corroded metal with a commercial rust remover.

2 Clean stubborn patches with very fine steel wool dipped in rust remover. Work in a circular motion.

3 Rinse off with water or wipe with a damp cloth. Dry thoroughly. Polish with impregnated wadding.

Pewter

Very badly corroded pewter should be left to the experts, especially if the object is old and valuable, but for less tarnished articles follow the treatment given here. Pewter does not rust as some metals do but can become dulled.

For regular cleaning clean with impregnated wadding.

WHAT YOU NEED
White spirit, Cloths
Wadding, Furniture wax
Car cleaner

1 For a soft polish, clean pewter first with white spirit. Apply furniture wax sparingly. Buff with a soft clean cloth.

2 For a higher shine, clean with white spirit then rub with car cleaning abrasive. Remove abrasive with soft cloth.

3 Polish with impregnated wadding; buff vigorously with a soft cloth. Apply a wax polish to protect ornaments.

Iron

When cleaning iron or steel, the final finish will depend on what best suits the object being restored. Old tools, for example, look well with a brown/black finish, preserved with wax.

For regular cleaning dust lacquered items. Rewax waxed iron. Reblack fireplaces.

WHAT YOU NEED
Wire brush, Oil, Emery paper, White spirit, Rust preventer

1 Remove rust with a wire brush. Remove stubborn rust with emery paper dipped in very light oil.

2 If painting, clean the surface with white spirit then apply rust preventive paint before the top coat.

3 Unpainted iron can be lacquered (below) or blacked with grate blacking. Apply with a cloth, then buff.

Lacquering

Few people have the time or the inclination to do the regular polishing that bright metals really need. Instead, a coat of lacquer can be applied to any of the metals on these two pages. Removing lacquer and relacquering is a fiddly, time consuming job but it saves regular cleaning.

WHAT YOU NEED
Gloves, Paint remover
Brushes, Lacquer

1 Remove old lacquer with paint stripper. Clean intricate bits with a brush. Clean as in Steps 1–3 (Brass).

2 Wash off the remains of metal polish with warm water and detergent. Rinse and dry with a soft cloth.

3 Apply the lacquer sparingly with a brush, making sure item is well covered and there are no drips.

Steel

Steel fenders and fire 'irons' are often to be found in junk shops in poor condition. Though they need time spent on them, they can make attractive additions to the home when properly cleaned.

Unless it is of the stainless variety, steel should be burnished regularly with very fine steel wool. This is a particu-larly effective treatment for steel knives which were often polished with emery powder.

For regular cleaning polish with impregnated wadding and a soft cloth. The cleaned surface can then be protected with a coating of white wax polish. If preferred, the surface can be given a protective coat of clear lacquer.

WHAT YOU NEED
Wire brush, Oil, Cloths
Fine emery paper
White spirit
Impregnated wadding
Wax polish

1   Clean off as much rust as you can, first using a wire brush to get into all the cracks. Then give the steel a good clean with light, penetrating oil on a soft cloth.

2   Clean the steel with oil and fine emery paper, rubbing hard enough to remove the rust but not hard enough to mark the surface. Wash off with white spirit. Dry with a clean cloth.

3   Wrap the item in paper to prevent it absorbing residual chemicals that may be in the airing cupboard and place it in the cupboard to dry out thoroughly.

4   Polish the dry steel with impregnated wadding to bring it up to a shine. Wipe off; buff with a clean cloth. Protect the surface with wax or lacquer (see Steps 1–3, page 129).

Aluminium

In today's homes aluminium can be used for window frames and kitchen unit trim, but its most popular use has always been for cooking utensils, particularly saucepans, because it is an especially good conductor of heat. It is also popular for tea-pots. The treatment shown here under General can be used on any aluminium in the home. Pans and teapots also suffer from the added problem of discolouration made by the contents —see below.

For regular cleaning use impregnated wadding, or for washable items scour with a scouring pad.

WHAT YOU NEED
Cream of tartar
Detergent
Soap-filled scouring pad
Impregnated wadding
Soft cloth, Borax

1 Wipe with hot water and mild detergent. Then use impregnated wadding or scouring pad. Rinse, dry well.

1 Place 15ml (1 tablespoon) cream of tartar in 575ml (1 pint) of water. Bring to the boil and simmer for a few minutes.

2 Empty out and wash the pan thoroughly in detergent and water. Use a scouring pad for stubborn areas.

1 To clean inside tannin-stained aluminium, fill with water to just above stain. Add 30ml (2 tablespoons) of borax.

2 Place the teapot over a low heat. Simmer over a low heat until stains flake and rise to surface.

3 Wash in detergent solution. Rub inside with scouring pad. Polish outside with impregnated wadding.

Repairing and cleaning wall coverings

Parting seams

Small tears

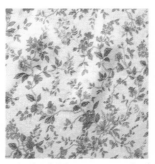

Air bubbles on washables and non-washables

Shabby wall coverings can be dramatically improved by simple repairs and cleaning, which is much less costly and time-consuming than having to repaper.

When working out how many rolls of paper you need, buy an extra one. It will be useful if you need to make a repair later on or if you make a mistake when wallpapering.

Preparation

Repairs to wall coverings involve patching and mending tears, eliminating air bubbles and replacing parted seams, treatment for which varies according to the type of wall covering used. The cause of a tear is usually obvious (toys, animals, sharp objects) but try to find the cause of air bubbles, corner damage and parting seams. They could be the signs of bad papering, drying out of adhesive or a mouldy or damp wall, all of which should be cured by the appropriate treatment or avoided in future.

Any wall surface to be repaired needs to be thoroughly cleaned, but stick down tears or parted seams (opposite) before cleaning or you could catch cleaning tools against them and make a more lengthy repair job than you had in the first place.

Repair problems

Different wall coverings usually present different repair problems. Vinyls and washables have a tough, slightly elastic surface that does not tear very easily, but the adhesive sometimes dries out, causing air bubbles and parting seams. Spongeable wall coverings have only a light protective finish and they tear easily. Non-washable wallpapers tear easily, especially when damp. Relief papers tear, and because they are heavy and usually painted, are also prone to parting seams. Specialist wall coverings, including hessian and other textiles, tear and then fray (unless you deal with them promptly), making the damage more serious and, unfortunately, more difficult to correct.

Large scratches

Damage to relief paper

Stains on textureds

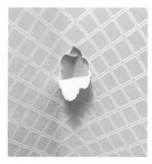

Corner damage

Parting seams

Apart from looking unsightly and gathering dirt, parting seams are a temptation to children, who prise them open, so causing more damage.

On vinyls, parting seams are caused by insufficient adhesive, central heating drying out the adhesive or dampness in the wall.

First tackle the cause of the problem then repair the seams as shown below.

On wallpaper and textured papers, parting seams should be dealt with as for tears.

WHAT YOU NEED
Mild detergent and cloth
Fungicidal wallpaper paste
Artist's paint brush
Clean cloth, Bucket
Small bowl and spoon

1 Clean the wall surface with a cloth that has been dampened with a mild detergent and water solution.

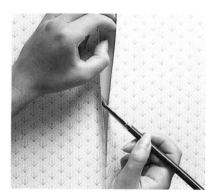

2 Apply fungicidal wallpaper paste generously with a fine brush to both of the vinyl seams where they separate.

3 Press the seams down firmly, using a clean, dry cloth. Wipe off excess adhesive with a damp cloth.

Tears

On wallpapers, repair tears as below. On vinyls, stick down small tears as for parting seams or patch as for textureds.

WHAT YOU NEED
Latex adhesive,
Clean, damp cloth

1 Remove old adhesive and dirt from the wall with a dampened cloth. Leave to dry. Then straighten out the damaged paper as much as you can, taking care not to tear or dirty it.

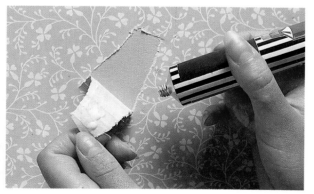

2 Apply a small dab of adhesive from the tube, and spread it evenly over the underside of the tear. Press down firmly into position, making sure that patterns and weaves match.

Air bubbles on vinyls and washables

These are very common and are due to the adhesive drying out or to damp or mould on the wall underneath. They look unsightly if left, but fortunately are easy to repair once the cause has been dealt with. Small air bubbles can be eliminated by making a simple horizontal slit in the paper, repasting it down toward the splits with the fingers. Larger air bubbles need the more drastic treatment described in the step-by-step sequence below.

WHAT YOU NEED
Sharp craft knife
Wallpaper paste
Artist's brush
Bowl, Spoon
Clean cloth

1 Using a sharp craft knife, find the centre of the air bubble and make slits in the shape of a cross.

2 Lift up the four flaps and paste carefully with adhesive, using a small artist's paint brush.

3 Press flap down firmly with a cloth and clean off the excess adhesive at once with a damp cloth.

Air bubbles on non-washables

Air bubbles on non-washable wallpapers are usually more noticeable than on vinyls, especially if the paper is painted.

WHAT YOU NEED
Wallpaper paste, Syringe, Cloth

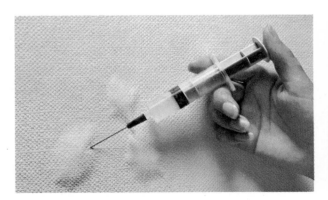

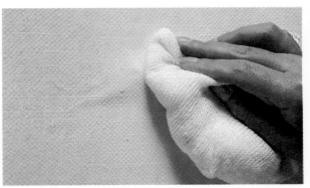

1 Fill a fine syringe with a medium solution of ordinary wallpaper adhesive. Inject gently into the bubble, slightly to one side of it, rather than directly into the centre.

2 Give the adhesive time to wet the paper thoroughly, then use a small cloth to flatten the bubble, working towards the hole. Don't push too hard or you will crease the paper.

Patching wallpapers

If the tears are large or stains still visible, use a matching patch. Make sure that colour on wall and new patch match—sometimes wall coverings fade when exposed to the light.

If you don't have matching material for a patch, consider camouflaging the damaged area with a picture.

WHAT YOU NEED
Latex adhesive
Clean cloth
Scissors
Flour paper (i.e. fine sandpaper)

1 Cut a piece of matching covering larger than the damage. After matching the pattern to the wall, carefully tear the edges of the patch to give a feathered effect.

2 Holding the patch over the damage, check for match. Coat the back of the patch with latex adhesive. Finally, press into position with cloth, matching carefully.

Patching relief wallpapers

Once painted, repairs on this type of wall covering are very successful—but never press heavily on the surface as it causes indentations.

WHAT YOU NEED
Paste, Brush, Filler, Flour paper, Paint

1 Follow Steps 1–4, page 136 as for textured coverings. Disguise gaps with fine filler. Clean off excess. Allow to dry.

2 Lightly sand off filler removing the rough surface from around the joins. Avoid damaging the raised pattern.

3 Brush off any filler dust then, with a small paint brush, apply matching paint over and around the patch.

Patching textured and vinyl wall coverings

When dealing with the thicker or more expensive textiles or vinyls, it is necessary to take out the damaged area completely and replace it with a new piece cut to fit. Textiles are slightly more difficult to repair than vinyl as the edges can fray but they can be held in place with a little glue. Make sure that you correctly match the pattern on vinyl, line up the weave on hessian and match horizontal lines on silk so as to disguise the patch as much as possible. Fabric wall coverings in particular fade over time and may become considerably lighter than a spare piece or roll that has been kept in a cupboard. To make sure that

colour matches perfectly on fabric wall coverings, leave a patch on a window sill to catch the sun for a few days until it fades to the colour that matches the original piece of wall covering still in situ.

WHAT YOU NEED
Pencil, Knife, Paste, Sticky tape,
Bowl, Artist's brush

1   Check for precise match in colour, pattern and texture. Hold up to damaged area matching piece slightly larger than the stain. Adjust for pattern match, trimming off excess.

2   Hold the piece temporarily in place with double-sided tape and, with knife against steel rule, make a clean cut through patch and bottom layer of the wall covering.

3   Remove the double-sided tape and set aside the new piece of wall covering. Then carefully remove the damaged piece of wall covering completely.

4   Paste the underside of the new piece. Hold the cut piece against the wall without pressing it down, checking for correct positioning again, then press down firmly.

Corner damage

When a length of wallpaper has been hung incorrectly into and out of a corner, it causes a weak point at which knocks can easily produce unsightly holes. Patching is never very successful here as the corner will always be a stress point. The best solution is to strip off the lengths of wallpaper leading into and out of the corner and hang new lengths, if you have them. Allow for this when buying wallpaper so you have an emergency supply. If you have only a small length of paper left, with a metal ruler and sharp craft knife, cut paper down the corner and stick the two cut edges down. This will leave a narrow strip of wall exposed all down the corner. Then use strips cut from the spare paper, pieced together lengthways to cover the exposed wall. Work slowly, making sure any pattern matches exactly.

WHAT YOU NEED
Tape measure, Decorator's large brush
Wallpaper scraper, Scissors
Suitable wallpaper paste and brush

1 Soak the paper first, then strip off the pieces of wallpaper leading into and out of the corner. Don't pull the paper too sharply when you are stripping it off.

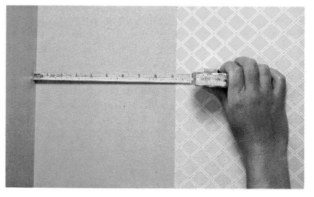

2 Measure the distance from the wallpaper seam into the corner at several points and add on 2.5cm to the longest measurement. Cut a matching length to this measurement.

3 Coat the length with the correct adhesive, position it against wall, matching up pattern with previous length. Press down, taking excess round corner. Fix well with decorator's brush.

4 Measure distance from previous seam into the corner. Cut a length of wallpaper to slightly wider than this. Position against wall and trim until pattern matches. Paste down.

Cleaning and stain removal

The appearance of nearly all wall coverings can be improved with an occasional vacuum clean using the soft bristle brush attachment on the cleaner. This light cleaning will not remove heavier dirt or stains, which need the more thorough cleaning described below.

Most modern wall coverings have a protective finish described as 'spongeable' or 'washable', but some may not be treated at all—the label on the roll should specify. These wall coverings can be protected from grease and dirt with a washable coating which can be cleaned. This is obtainable from wallpaper or DIY shops.

General cleaning

Always keep care labels when you buy wall coverings, or ask retailer's advice on cleaning. Test-clean a small, hidden area before you begin.

Vinyls and washables usually have a tough, impervious finish, so they can be scrubbed with a solution of hot water and washing-up liquid and a stiff brush. Always work from the bottom upwards, at the same time cleaning dirty streaks which could spoil the cleaned area. Rinse with a clean rag and warm water.

Spongeable wall coverings should never be cleaned with harsh abrasive or stiff brushes. Use a sponge soaked in warm, mild washing-up liquid solution. Wring it out, then lightly wipe across the dirty surface. Rinse with clear, warm water and clean sponge, taking care not to soak the wall.

Non-washable wallpapers should never be dampened. Dust with a dry, soft brush.

Relief papers can be dusted with a dry sponge. Do not use water on unpainted papers as it would soften and therefore damage the surface. Painted relief decorations can be sponged with a weak solution of washing-up liquid and warm water, then rinsed with cold water. Never scrub the surface as such rough treatment could cause permanent indentations in the paper.

Specialist wall coverings include hessian and other textiles. Treat with great care. Test on hidden area, then dab lightly at dirty spots with warm water and soap flakes, with a well wrung out sponge. Or try a 50–50 solution of methylated spirits and water, but test for colour runs, shrinkage and possible tearing.

If in doubt, call in a professional cleaner or get in touch with the manufacturers of the wall covering for advice.

Removing stains

First identify the stain and wall covering and test the method in a hidden area. If you cannot remove the stain, disguise it with a patch—tear rather than cut wallpaper for a softer edge.

Removing stains on washables and vinyls is straightforward since the protective finish should prevent bad stains. Light stains can be removed with hot water and washing-up liquid. Remove bad marks from vinyls—but not 'spongeables'— with a nylon brush and scouring powder. Solvent cleaners damage the plasticized finish.

Removing stains on non-washables is difficult as water, detergent or abrasives damage the surface. The most common stains can, however, be removed as described.

Felt-tipped pen

Place a spare piece of cloth underneath the stains and dab the marks with methylated spirits applied on a clean cloth. Don't rub the mark; it could easily spread further. Place blotting paper over mark. Iron with a warm iron, or use dry foam stain remover.

Ink

Immediately blot off as much as you can with paper tissues, placing spare tissues underneath to absorb as much ink as possible from the underside. Don't rub as this will spread the stain. Dab at remains with methylated spirits on a cotton-wool bud. Spray on dry foam cleaner, leave to dry to a powder, then gently brush off. Disguise difficult stains with a patch. On children's clothes, fun motto patches can often be used to great effect.

Pencil marks

Remove with soft India rubber, gently rubbing across the mark. As the rubber becomes dirty, use the clean side to avoid re-distributing the marks.

Wine

Blot immediately with tissues or paper kitchen towels to soak up liquid. Dab on talcum powder, leave for a few minutes, then lightly brush off with a very soft brush. This will remove most or all of the stain without damaging the paper. If any stain remains, dab on a little glycerine, but do not oversoak the paper or it may tear.

Lengthening the life of your carpet

Carpets and rugs not only create an atmosphere of warmth, cosiness, even luxury, in the home, but they also represent a large financial investment. Even in the most careful families, it is difficult to avoid subjecting the carpet to varying degrees of wear. Some areas, such as doorways or heavy traffic areas between rooms and stairs, often wear thin in patches, while the floor covering in the rest of the room is still perfectly serviceable.

A carpet can be patched or relaid to improve its appearance and extend its life (see steps below). For this reason, when buying a new carpet, ask the fitter not to throw away the off-cuts. Keep larger pieces for repairs and use small pieces when matching other soft furnishings or when choosing wall coverings and paint.

Safety

Quite apart from improving the appearance of the carpet, safety is an important reason for making repairs. Worn carpets or badly executed joins in doorways and at the top of staircases are particularly hazardous. Surprisingly, most accidents happen in the home and defective floor coverings are a major cause of accidents, especially to people over the age of 65. The methods which follow can be used to eliminate these hazards and make your home much safer for the family. The steps cover repairing burn marks, patching worn areas, fitting a threshold strip and relaying a stair carpet.

New from old

As well as smartening up the appearance of the room and improving safety in the home by repairing existing carpet, the methods which follow can be used to adapt old carpet to a new location. Once you have mastered the process of cutting out the worn areas and joining up pieces of carpet, you will be able to move carpet from an old home to a new home, from one room to another or to make a smart 'new' floor covering from a secondhand carpet discarded by its previous owner. (Auction rooms, rather than junk shops, are a good source for these bargains.)

Carpets are easily damaged or stained. Learn how to repair and spread the wear to prolong their life.

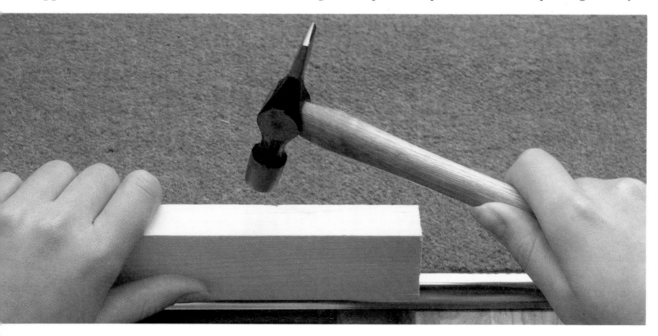

How to repair burn marks

A small hole or scorch mark, caused by a cigarette burn or flying spark from an open fire, is easy to disguise on a woollen carpet. Simply replace the scorched tufts with others from a hidden area. A burn is more difficult to deal with on synthetic-fibre carpets as these melt, making it difficult to remove the tufts. Patch the area instead (see pages 141–2).

WHAT YOU NEED
Latex adhesive, Piece of card
Manicure stick, Artist's paintbrush or similar sharp instrument
Hammer, Nail scissors
Damp cloth, in case of spillage

1 Tease out scorched fibres from the burnt area, then tease out matching fibres from another area of the carpet, where it will not be obvious.

2 Using a manicure stick or the wooden end of a paintbrush, place a tiny dab of latex adhesive into the bottom of the burn hole. Apply adhesive to the bottom half of each tuft.

3 Leave adhesive to dry, then push tufts carefully into position with the end of a clean, pointed stick. The tufts will stick instantly to the dried adhesive in the hole.

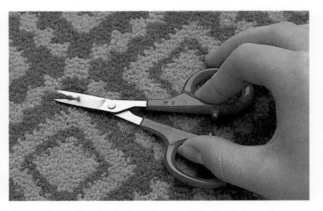

4 When the hole has been filled with tufts, hammer down to ensure a strong bond. If any of the tufts stand proud of the surrounding carpet area, trim with nail scissors until level.

How to patch worn areas

Worn areas of carpet can usually be patched with good results. You will need to find a perfect piece of carpet of suitable size and pattern to use as a replacement. If there are no off-cuts available, it is often possible to find a large enough area of carpet hidden away under a piece of furniture where it will not matter if carpet is cut away. Cut the initial patch larger than the repair and cut through both patch and carpet.

There are two techniques. The first, in which the patch is fitted from the top, will be necessary if the carpet is fitted, and advisable if it is patterned, so as to ensure a perfect pattern match. Use the second method—fitting the patch from the back—for plain, loose-laid carpets.

> **WHAT YOU NEED**
> **Sharp craft knife, Latex adhesive**
> **Hessian carpet seaming tape (or hessian)**
> **Brown paper, Scissors, Metal ruler**

Patching from the top

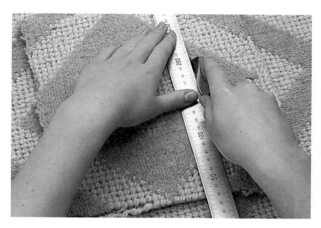

1 Having cut a replacement piece, lay patch over worn area—matching pattern and direction of pile—and cut through *both* layers with sharp craft knife outside damaged area.

2 Dab latex adhesive on to the edges of the patch to prevent it from fraying. Apply sparingly, making sure the adhesive comes only half way up the pile. Leave to dry.

3 Cut a piece of brown paper slightly larger than the hole, and push it through the hole to lie flat between underlay and carpet. This will prevent adhesive from sticking to underlay.

4 Cut four strips of carpet tape, slightly longer than sides of patch. Insert them, hessian side up, through hole—half beneath carpet, half exposed. Coat them with adhesive.

5 Apply adhesive to the back of the patch. Leave until nearly dry, then align patch carefully over hole—matching pattern and pile direction——and press gently into position.

6 Pinch the edges of the patch to tease the fibres of the patch in with those of the surrounding carpet. Tap the edges of the patch with a hammer to ensure a solid bond.

Patching from the back

1 Follow Steps 1 and 2 (page 141). Cut a patch of seaming tape slightly larger than patch. Apply adhesive to tape and back of patch. Leave to dry, then press together.

2 Turn carpet over, and apply a border of adhesive around hole. Leave to dry, then press patch into place. Lay a piece of brown paper on floor; relay carpet, and repeat Step 6.

How to fit a threshold strip

When a carpet is fitted in a doorway, people often merely tuck under the carpet and tack it in place. This looks messy, and can lead to the carpet edge being kicked up. Metal edging strips across the threshold of a room provide a neat finish, as well as a secure fixing, helping to eliminate accidents caused by tripping over protruding corners.

Threshold strips are available in a wide variety of profiles for use in different positions with various types of floor coverings. The range includes double binder bars, for use where two carpets meet in a doorway, and cover strips, for use where a carpet in one room butts up to vinyl flooring in the adjoining room.

There are single edgings for fixing carpets, vinyl and linoleum on one side only. These should be used when the floor covering in one room meets ceramic floor tiles or a polished wooden floor in the next (see Steps below).

Special edgings are available for foam-backed carpets. Alternatively, use ordinary edging strip, following Steps 1, 2, 4 and 5, but trimming back the foam backing so that the full thickness does not overlap the strip.

The edging strips are sold in standard 813mm lengths, which are slightly wider than the average doorway, so as to allow for cutting to fit. They are available in aluminium, solid brass, and a brass-look finish.

WHAT YOU NEED

Tape measure
Metal edging strip of appropriate profile
Small hacksaw (to cut strip if necessary)
12mm nails, Carpet tacks
Hammer
Epoxy or contact adhesive (if sticking
  strip to concrete)
Sharp craft knife
Pencil
Metal ruler
Block of wood (for protecting strip from
  the hammer, and protecting carpet
whilst
  trimming)
Piece of cloth (for protecting strip whilst
  cutting to length)

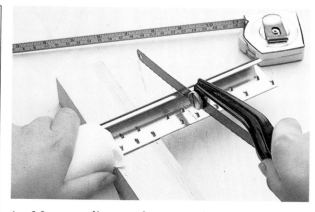

1 Measure distance between door posts, and mark cutting line on top of threshold strip. Wrap a cloth round the strip, lay strip on a block of wood, and cut to fit, using a hacksaw.

2 Nail strip to floor in appropriate place, hammering nails through holes provided. If the floor is concrete, stick edging strip in place with contact or epoxy adhesive.

3 Using a sharp craft knife, trim underlay to butt up with the edge of the base plate. Tack down the underlay before you start, to prevent it from slipping as you cut.

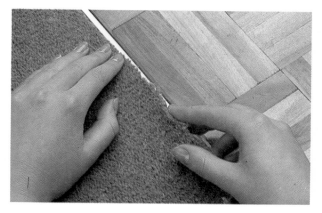

4 Trim carpet so that it will fit into the recess of the edging strip. Tuck the carpet into the recess using your fingers—or use a sharp stick or wide chisel.

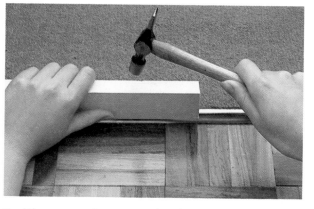

5 To secure the carpet in place, tap down the flange along its length, using a piece of wood to protect the metal. Use a small hammer for greater accuracy.

How to spread wear on the stairs

Stair carpets receive heaviest wear on the front edge of each step and no wear at all on the riser, so it makes good sense to lift and relay the stair carpet at regular intervals.

Ideally, stair carpets should be moved a few centimetres up or down every 12 months. Most carpet fitters allow for this by laying the carpet with a surplus length turned under on the top step or bottom riser, or with a double layer on the top step. Carpets are now usually fitted on stair carpet grippers which cannot be seen in use as they hold the carpet firmly from the back. Your stairs will probably either be fitted with a metal stair carpet gripper, or with wooden gripper strips. Both types are shown below left.

Carpet grippers

Metal stair carpet grippers comprise an angled metal bar with rows of strong protruding teeth. When in position, fixed in the angle between the step and the riser of each stair, the gripper holds the carpet in position and also enables it to be lifted off, moved and replaced with ease. In this case, the underlay runs beneath the carpet grippers, but with wooden gripper strips the bare wood of the stair is left exposed between the strips.

Lifting the carpet

When lifting the carpet, note first how it was fixed at the top and bottom. If using surplus from the bottom, turn under the appropriate length at the top before fixing. If taking surplus from the top, make the turning a few centimetres less than it was originally. If the carpet is already worn on the step edges, first decide whether the damaged areas will be less noticeable on the steps or on the risers and adapt position of carpet accordingly.

If the staircase has a turn in it—and each winder is not fitted separately—use carpet tacks to make tucks on the winders and then continue on the grippers, as before, to the bottom. If each winder is fitted separately, you will not be able to move the pieces of carpet.

Carpet on stairs is especially prone to wear.

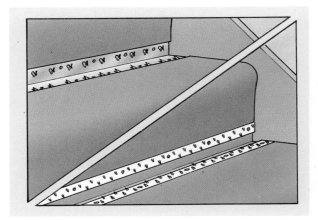

Metal gripper bars (a) or wooden gripper strips (b) are now normally fitted when new caprets are laid on the stairs.

WHAT YOU NEED
**Carpet tacks, 12mm nails, Hammer
Metal bolster or plywood block (if metal
stair grippers are fitted)**

1 Pull up the stair carpet, and check whether the excess has been positioned on the top or bottom step. Roll up the carpet from the bottom and reposition, decreasing or increasing top fold.

2 If you are decreasing top fold, cut some underlay from the bottom riser, which will now be excess, and tack it on to top step, to fit flush against edge of new fold (see below left).

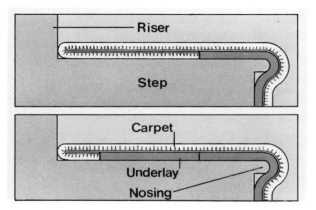

Decreasing the turn on the top stair means that the underlay must be cut away from below the carpet to fit. If increasing fold, cut underlay back.

3 Having decreased fold, lay carpet on top step, and tack down. Start with the centre tack, and move outwards in alternate directions, to ensure equal tension across step.

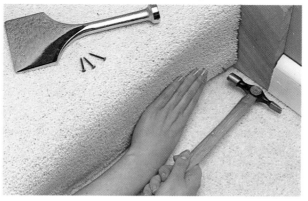

4 Pull carpet across step, and down over the nosing. Make sure that it is pulled taut, then punch it into the gulley between stair grippers with bolster. Run bolster along crease.

5 Continue downwards unrolling as you go, until you reach the bottom step. Make new fold in carpet (increase if you decreased at top), and tack down at bottom edge.

Mending broken china

Breaking a plate or some other article of chinaware can be a daunting experience if you cannot buy a replacement, or it has a special sentimental value. Fortunately, you can repair or restore most broken or cracked china without too much difficulty. The keys to success are patience and extreme care, paying particular attention to keeping the china clean throughout the process.

If you have valuable pieces, it is not a good idea to repair these yourself. Instead, take the broken item to an antique shop and ask their advice.

Tools and equipment
Ideally, when you break or chip chinaware it should be repaired immediately, while the edges are still clean. If this isn't possible, place the pieces in a box or plastic bag for safe-keeping until you are able to carry out the repair.

The best adhesive for china repairs is the type that has two elements—an epoxy resin that you mix with an accompanying hardener to give a strong, heat-proof bond. The two should be mixed together in equal amounts. When mixed, the adhesive looks yellowish, so in most cases you will need to add a small amount of titanium dioxide or fine talcum powder to whiten it so that it blends in with the china.

When you first use the adhesive, only mix up small amounts as you will find you are fairly slow on the first repair, and may not finish before the adhesive has hardened. At a room temperature of 18–24°C the mixture will remain usable for about two hours. Both of the surfaces to be bonded together should always be cleaned with acetone (nail polish remover), before you apply a tiny amount of adhesive to each, carefully following instructions on the container.

General techniques
All parts to be repaired must be scrupulously clean. Wash them first in warm soapy water, rinse them and leave to dry thoroughly. If you are restoring an antique piece, it may be necessary to soak it first, to loosen dirt from old cracks.

It is not necessary to go out and buy sophisticated tools or equipment for simple repairs. Most can be carried out with items found around

You don't have to be an expert to repair breaks in china. Mending even complex breaks just takes a little patience and a lot of care.

the home, like nail polish remover, a general purpose epoxy resin and plasticine.

Where you are regluing old breaks, the old glue must be removed first. You can either soak the china in very hot water for 20 minutes or bake in a warm oven for 30 minutes to loosen the glue. Then remove the dissolved glue with a clean cloth; it is important to remove all of it.

When repairing china always work in the daytime and preferably near a window. The temperature should be fairly warm, to allow the adhesive to run freely, then set fairly quickly on the repair.

Whatever kind of repair you do, it is important to plan the work carefully before you begin and make sure that all the necessary tools and materials are to hand. Work at a clean, firm table or bench, which can be left undisturbed until the repairs are completed. Put down plenty of clean newspapers around the work-table and spread it with a clean, old cloth to protect surfaces and make sure the area is kept dust free.

Once the china has been repaired, place it in a secure support where it can be left untouched while the adhesive sets—it can take up to three days to reach full strength. The instructions leaflet or label should tell you the correct timing. See page 149 for examples of supports.

How to mend simple breaks

One of the easiest repairs is gluing two pieces together where there is a clean break.

Before you begin, position the support close to where you will be working. Plates and saucers are best held in a vertical position while the adhesive sets. Use ordinary household nail varnish remover as a solvent for cleaning the pieces prior to gluing. Lay plenty of clean newspapers around the work surface and a clean, old cloth on it. Keep your tools and hands as clean as possible and avoid moving the item for three days.

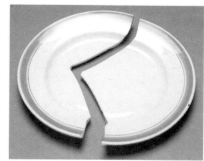

This plate had a single large break and could easily be mended. Afterwards it looked as good as new.

WHAT YOU NEED
Mild household detergent
Plastic bowl
Cleaning cloths (lint-free)
Epoxy resin and hardener
Ceramic tile
Wooden lollipop sticks
Titanium dioxide
Acetone
Cotton wool
Fine sand
Safety razor blade
Fine wet and dry paper
Deep bowl, Steel nail-file

1 Give broken pieces a thorough wash in a plastic bowl of warm water and mild household detergent. Rinse. When dry, clean along the broken edges with acetone.

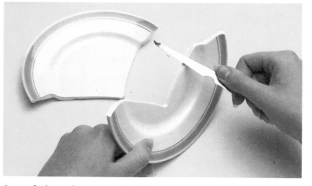

2 If the plate was broken some time ago, slightly roughen the edges to provide a good 'key' for the repair, by carefully filing across the breaks with a steel nail-file.

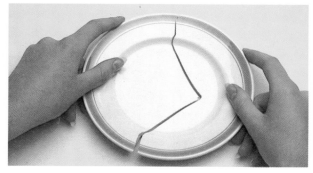

3 At this stage, check that the pieces fit neatly together and that there are no deep chips or holes that need filling. Fit the pieces together on a clean surface.

4 Mix epoxy resin and hardener on tile or glass, using lollipop stick. Squeeze out equal parts and mix together, adding enough titanium dioxide to whiten as required.

5 Apply very thin coats of adhesive on a cocktail stick to each edge. Press pieces together firmly and hold for two minutes. Remove surplus adhesive with a razor blade.

6 A bowl filled with fine sand makes a firm support for vertical items. Carefully wedge repair into the sand, leave for three days. Rub back any ridges with wet and dry paper.

How to mend multiple breaks

These require extra patience and time because it is essential to build up the repair gradually—section by section. It is also very important first to assemble the pieces and number each one in clockwise order before gluing them together. The repair will need a particularly secure support to protect the china while the adhesive 'cures'. Before starting the repair, you will need to prepare a support, as shown on the opposite page.

Even multiple breaks can be successfully mended although they require a little patience.

1 Wash, dry and clean all pieces as in Step 1, page 147. Carefully fit all the pieces together on a clean surface. When completed, strap together with pieces of sticky tape.

2 To make sure that you glue all the pieces together in the correct order, use an erasable marker to number each piece clearly, working in a clockwise sequence.

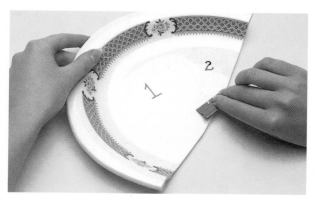

3   Having mixed the adhesive and titanium dioxide as in Step 4, page 147, remove sticky tape from pieces 1 and 2. Clean with acetone. When dry, apply adhesive to edges of 1 and 2.

4   Never allow surplus adhesive to harden on the repair. After pressing two edges together, carefully remove excess with a razor blade. Leave supported for at least six hours.

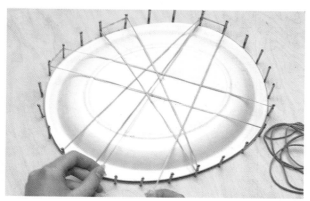

5   Remove repaired piece from its support, and fit next two pieces to the repair, following Steps 3 and 4. Place back in vertical support for another six hours.

6   When all pieces have been assembled step by step, place face downwards on to prepared wooden base. Stretch rubber bands over nails and leave repair for twenty-four hours.

Some suggested supports

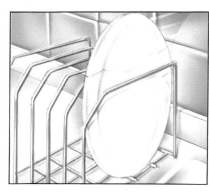

Kitchen plate or draining rack is ideal for holding vertical repairs.

To secure large china repairs, a drawer can be carefully closed against the repair and held in place, safely wedged in plasticine.

149

How to mend cracks

Cracks tend to fall into two main categories: those on glazed surfaces on dirty, old china, and those caused when a whole piece is damaged.

A liberal swabbing with hydrogen peroxide, applied on cotton wool, removes glazing cracks. Stubborn ones may need further treatment before they disappear. Always wear protective gloves.

Deep cracks need to be repaired before they can spread. Kaolin mixed into the adhesive acts as putty/filler. It also disguises the cracks.

An old dinner service can be given a new lease of life with hydrogen peroxide, a bleaching agent which disguises cracks on glazed surfaces.

WHAT YOU NEED
Mild household detergent
Plastic bowl, Clean cloths
Rubber gloves
Hydrogen peroxide
Epoxy resin and hardener
Ceramic tile, Kaolin
Cotton wool
Acetone (nail polish remover)
Wooden lollipop sticks
Fine wet and dry paper
Support

1 Thoroughly wash the plate in a warm, soapy solution—and then leave it to soak in plastic bowl for at least 12 hours. Dry thoroughly with a clean, lint-free cloth.

2 Clean along crack with a dab of acetone on cotton wool. Prepare 'putty' by mixing equal parts of adhesive and hardener, then add a little kaolin to give a putty consistency.

3 Use a clean wooden lollipop stick to apply a fine layer of this 'putty' along the crack, building it up along the crack to slightly above the surface of the item.

4 Having placed the plate in a support for four hours, level back putty, using small pieces of wet and dry paper rubbed carefully across the crack. Avoid scratching glaze.

How to mend broken handles

When a handle breaks off, usually the break is quite clean and therefore easy to repair. You must, however, consider the usage to which repaired handles will be subjected in the future.

While the recommended adhesive is heat-proof, some heavy repaired items subjected to dishwashers, and hot ovens, can eventually break again, possibly causing an accident. If you don't want to get rid of it, the alternative is to keep the item for decorative use only for safety's sake.

When a handle breaks off the two stubs are normally left intact. These can be used as bases for repairing the handles.

WHAT YOU NEED
Mild household detergent
Plastic bowl
Clean cloths
Cotton wool
Acetone (nail polish remover)
Epoxy resin and hardener
Cocktail sticks
Ceramic tile
Plasticine
Rubber bands
Safety razor blade
Fine wet and dry paper

1 Wash the handle and cup in warm soapy water as in Step 1, page 147. When dry, clean broken surfaces with a dab of acetone on a piece of cotton wool.

2 Replace the broken handle on the two stubs, checking they fit properly, then stretch rubber bands across mug and handle to hold them in position while you carry out the repair.

3 Lay mug on its side and press into a bed of soft plasticine. Lift one side of handle, apply mixed adhesive to both stub and handle, press down. Repeat for other side.

4 Having removed surplus adhesive with razor blade, working across break, press on to and leave in plasticine for 12 hours. Rub back any ridges with fine wet and dry paper.

Index

Adhesives
  removing 120
  using 16, 19
Antique dealer, buying
    from 8
Auctions 8

Blowtorch, using 24, 25
Borders
  geometric 58–60
  painting 54, 55
  self-adhesive 57
  templates 60
  use of 56

Carpet
  burn marks 140
  repairs 138
  stairs, spreading wear
    on 144
  threshold strip 142
  worn areas, patching 141
Chairs
  armchair, renewing 95–106
  arm fabric, fitting 106
  back pad, upholstering
    93, 94
  cutting plan for fabric
    99–101
  dining, renovating 82
  drop-in seat, replacing
    82–86
  frame, parts of 98
  inner arm cover 101
  measuring for materials 98
  outside arm fabric 105
  second-hand 12
  sprung seat, replacing
    87–92
Chest, second-hand 12
China, mending
  breaks in 147–149
  cracks in 150
  equipment 146
  handles, broken 151
  techniques 147
  tools 146
Clamping joints 16
Cupboards, second-hand 12

Distemper, removing 52
Dowelling 17

Fabrics
  stains see Stains
  upholstery see Upholstery
Frames 12
Furniture

Art Deco 11
Arts and Crafts 10
Art Nouveau 11
breaks 19
dismantling 16
Edwardian 10
late Victorian 10
loose joints, mending 21
mid-Victorian 9
modern movement 11
Regency 8
renovation 6
repairs 16–22
second-hand 8–15
stripped 27
unsteady legs 17

Headboard, making
    107–114
  button pattern 109
  materials 108, 109
  recovering 107
Hot air stripper, using on
    skirtings and doors 25
House sales, buying in 8

Ink stains, removing
    121, 138

Junk shops, buying in 8

Marbling
  blending and veining 37
  colour 37
  finishes 36
  finishing 38
  practising 36
  preparation 39
  scumble glaze 38
  softening brush 36
  stippling 37
  surface, preparing 40
  techniques 41
  types of 39
Metals, caring for
  aluminium 131
  brass 128
  copper 128
  finish, restoring 125
  identifying 125–127
  iron 129
  lacquering 129
  pewter 128
  producing 125
  protection of 127
  restoration 126
  safety precautions 126
  steel 130
Mirrors 12

Newspapers, buying from 8

Painting 45
  borders 45
  distemper, removing 52

emulsion paint 53
preparation 46, 47
quantities 53
starting 52
stencils see Stencils
Papering see Wall coverings
Paste stripper 24, 28
Plaster, crumbling 51
Powder stripper 24

Sanding 24, 31
Sandpaper 30
Solvent paint remover
    24, 26
Stains, removing 115–120
  adhesives 120
  chocolate 121
  coffee 122
  ink 121, 138
  lipstick 122
  oil 123
  pencil 138
  red wine 123, 138
  rust 124
  tar 124
  wall coverings, on 138
Stencils
  cutting 65
  materials 63
  methods 65–68
  patterns 64
  preparation 63
  surfaces 69
  using 62

Tables
  breaks, mending 19
  second-hand 12

Upholstery
  back-pad 93, 94
  completion of 102
  cutting plan for fabric
    99–101
  drop-in seat, replacing
    82–86
  headboard see Headboards
  materials 83, 88, 96
  quantities 83
  second-hand furniture 14
  sprung seat, replacing
    87–92
  tools 88

Wall coverings
  air bubbles 134
  ceiling, on 79
  cleaning 132–138
  corner damage 137
  cutting lengths 73
  doors, round 77
  equipment 70, 71
  hanging 70, 78
  lining 73

paste-the-wall 75
pasting 74
patching 135–136
putting up 76
quantities 72
ready-pasted 75
removing 47
seams 133
stain removal 138
stripping 48–49
tears 133
vinyl 48
windows, round 78
Wallpaper see Wall
  coverings
Wall surface
  crumbling plaster 51
  filling 50
  mould 51
  preparing 47, 72
  textured 48
Wood
  bleaching 29, 30, 33
  filling 31, 34
  refinishing 29–35
  repairing 132–138
  sanding 24, 30
  staining 29, 31, 35
  stencilling 69
  stopping 31, 34
  stripping 23–28
  surface preparing 29
  varnishing 32, 35
Woodworm 14, 15